D0731988

THE VALUE
OF WEEDS

THE VALUE OF WEEDS

Ann Cliff

WITHDRAWN

THE CROWOOD PRESS

First published in 2017 by
The Crowood Press Ltd
Ramsbury, Marlborough
Wiltshire SN8 2HR

www.crowood.com

© Ann Cliff 2017

All rights reserved. No part of this publication may be reproduced or transmitted in any form or by any means, electronic or mechanical, including photocopy, recording, or any information storage and retrieval system, without permission in writing from the publishers.

British Library Cataloguing-in-Publication Data
A catalogue record for this book is available from the British Library.

ISBN 978 1 78500 278 6

Typeset by Jean Cussons Typesetting, Diss, Norfolk

Printed and bound in India by Replika Press Pvt Ltd

CONTENTS

ACKNOWLEDGEMENTS

My thanks are due to the many people who have given me help and encouragement in putting this book together.

Peter and Irene Foster of Lime Tree Farm, my brother and sister-in-law, have generously shared their knowledge and experience of converting the farm for wildlife conservation. I'm grateful for their hospitality over many years, including cups of Irene's hawthorn berry tea. In spite of the fact that much of my time is now spent in Australia, they keep me in touch with Lime Tree and the natural world in Yorkshire. (Irene made the weed frittata featured in the recipe chapter and it was excellent.)

Jill Askham and Martin Varley have been with me on many field trips and have provided company, equipment, transport and refreshments. On cross-country walks we have tracked down weeds, fallen into bogs, taken photographs of lovely wild flowers, and enjoyed the varied countryside of the Yorkshire Dales.

John Earnshaw read the 'Weeds for Health' chapter of the book and offered valuable insights into his profession: he is a scientific herbalist who likes to collect his own plant material.

Norman Bush gave me help with the chapter on dyeing, and kindly modelled his jacket creation, dyed with lichen. Norman is a craft teacher who delights in foraging for weeds. He also lent me books from his eclectic collection.

Tony and Wendy Robins provided the photograph of hand hoeing, and explained how they control weeds on their organic farm.

I am grateful to the staff at Artison craft workshop at Masham, North Yorkshire, and especially tutor Jess Wilkinson, for insights into the craft of willow weaving and her creative use of 'weeds'.

Michael Harrison kindly supplied the photograph of duckweed.

Thanks as always to my husband Neville, for his support.

Ann Cliff

INTRODUCTION

Can you tolerate weeds? It may be an acquired skill: we have been fighting them for thousands of years and it may not be easy to give up. In conventional thinking weeds are the enemy, and sometimes this is true. However, many weeds are beneficial, even essential, and that's what this book is about.

Weeds are rascals, sometimes villains, cheeky survivors, enjoying life wherever they can find a roothold in the earth. They are often a neglected resource in gardens and on farms – or wherever they grow. Weeds are not always the enemy of cultivation. In spite of everything we throw at them they forgive us and thrive, contributing biomass, healing the scars we inflict on the earth, and giving us food and medicine. Some of them light up our lives with beauty.

What's the definition of a weed? The word comes from old English 'weod' meaning grass or herb, but it has come to mean a plant we despise.

Don't be ashamed of your weeds – or not all of them. Only a few are a real menace, a matter for elimination, while many weeds have value. 'Weed' is a negative label, bestowed upon a plant because it's been rejected by our culture. A plant's status can vary over time and location; some of our despised weeds were once valued vegetables, and some are still cultivated in other parts of the world.

A weed may be growing in the wrong place, or it meets with disapproval because of its frightening fecundity. We're scared it will take over – and this can happen. Our food plants depend on us to help them grow in spite of weed competition, and conventional food production demands the elimination of weeds.

Some weeds are so beautiful that we forgive them for appearing unexpectedly. Honeysuckle (*Lonicera periclymenum*), pushing through a hedge with long trailing vines, drenches the evening air with fragrance. This is Shakespeare's 'luscious woodbine', a favourite hedge plant, the creamy flowers tinged with red and deepening to orange as they fade away. The two lips of the flowers form a tube that is much visited by long-tongued moths at night from May to August.

Honeysuckle is essential to the survival of a spectacular gliding butterfly, the white admiral,

Honeysuckle is a wild climber.

Ground elder.

in forested areas. Black with white bands on the upper side of the wings, this butterfly lays its eggs on honeysuckle leaves, which provide food for its caterpillars. As we will see, many weeds are important to our wildlife.

Of course there are nuisance weeds. Many of us battle with ground elder (*Aegopodium podagraria*), of which more later. This weed is invasive and very hard to eliminate. Any plant not native to a natural environment can be an undesirable influence because it can change the balance of an ecosystem. Ground elder, or gout weed, has been moved round the world as an ornamental plant, or as a vegetable or medicine. It is a nuisance, but it's also good to eat.

Another such invader is Indian or Himalayan balsam (*Impatiens glandulifera*), a plant introduced to Britain in 1839 for its looks. It grows rampant along some of our river systems, changing the ecology of the river banks. Many other plants were brought to Britain by plant hunters looking for new fashions in gardening. Originally much admired, some have become weeds.

In the case of weeds introduced from other countries, the natural controls that keep these plants in check in their native lands are often not present in the UK, which is one reason why they have become a problem. DEFRA's list of the worst invasive plants demonstrates this (*see* the section on weed safety for some of them).

However, it's not all bad news. In some circles there is a fresh mindset about the plants that surround us, as we realize that many weeds have virtues – but it's hard to give up our orderly ways. It's easy to spray out of existence any plants that grow uninvited in the wrong place, especially when they threaten to compete with our carefully nurtured cultivated plants. Weeds are untidy. Trying to keep our gardens, farms and window boxes as neat as those in glossy magazines, we also have to compete with friends, neighbours and television gurus. Our standards in Britain seem to have been set by the beautiful gardens of stately homes, tended by armies of gardeners in the past.

We like to spend time outdoors in manicured spaces, but to save work there is so much paving and gravel that few plants survive – and weeds, of course, are banned.

So what happens when we get rid of sprays and think about weeds in a more positive way? For a start, we save money and cut down our reliance on chemicals. We stop releasing potentially harmful substances into the environment, and avoid the risk of contaminating our fresh garden produce. We help bees, among many beneficial insects including other pollinators, to survive. We

Indian balsam.

start to notice some fascinating inhabitants of the plant world.

In this book we will look at weeds to appreciate their benefits and see how they can be useful to us. Many of them are also classified as herbs and have a list of traditional uses, some of which have been verified by science. It's exciting to see what food and medicine is volunteering to grow in your area.

If you have no garden, there's a lot of scope for finding useful wild plants on public and private land of various kinds: byways, hedges and woods (but don't pick plants on National Trust property, and don't uproot any plant without the permission of the landowner). Canal banks can be quiet sources of useful weeds. Farmers are usually happy for you to harvest weeds along the edges of fields and on rights of way, providing you observe the country code. Autumn is a good time: look

for crab apples, blackberries, rosehips and elderberries, all common and all growing wild in old hedges. Crab apples are sour little wild cousins of cultivated apples, delicious when made into crab apple jelly.

There is a sensible middle ground, somewhere between killing all volunteer plants and embracing the lot. Weeds have to be managed, to prevent their vigorous growth swamping our crops in field and garden and changing natural ecosystems in the wild. Sometimes they can be allowed to grow beside cultivated plants, to the benefit of the crop.

It may take courage to allow weeds to grow on your patch, but it's likely to become more usual in the future. Weeds worldwide are attracting a lot of interest. They are becoming more respectable. Instead of apologizing, in the future you'll be able to point to the bees and butterflies enjoying your volunteer plants.

Many weeds that were formerly cultivated have jumped over the garden wall and taken to the wild. Aggressive garden plants such as the periwinkle are included in the book because they can easily become weeds, taking every chance to sneak into beds of other plants and sometimes smothering the rightful occupants. Many of them are useful and can be harvested rather than killed, but the real marauders have to be kept under control.

One section of this book summarizes a few of the ways in which weeds have traditionally been used as medicine. In the past, health care was not available for many people, because they couldn't afford it or they lived too far from a town, and they often had to use what remedies they could find. Sometimes the women of the family were guardians of herbal lore, or there might be whole families who were known for their knowledge and skill. Wales seems to have been a place where folk medicine flourished, as in Myddfai where there were famous herb doctors in medieval times.

Happily in our own day some of these folk medicines, despised for centuries by doctors, have been proved by science to be effective. Attitudes to plants gradually changed when vitamins were discovered, starting in 1912. It had been found previously that vegetables and fruit prevented scurvy, the terrible disease that killed sailors on long voyages, but nobody knew until the twentieth century that scurvy is caused by a deficiency of vitamin C.

Our weeds represent the cottager's store cupboard, and also the poor folks' pharmacy. For health foods and for minor ailments, for drinks and dyes, they are still there, waiting to be used if you care to try them. And more people are doing so: there are signs that weeds are going upmarket. Foraging for wild foods has become popular in many parts of the world. Some foraging courses, arranged to educate beginners, are quite sophisticated 'wild food weekends', which may include trips away to hotels and gourmet chefs.

Bees on blackberry flowers.

Ringlet butterfly.

More respectability for scallywag weeds must be a good thing.

Wildlife could not exist without weeds for food and shelter. The more wild corners we can leave for weeds both large and small, the more habitats are preserved. Honeybees and bumblebees are valuable pollinators and they need weeds to support them, just to take one example; flower meadows are important for their survival.

Butterflies need weeds. The ringlet butterfly is quite common and is one of the few that flies on overcast days; it likes damp grasses on which to lay eggs.

It has been hard to allocate any one particular place in this book to our most useful weeds: naturally enough they keep popping up again and again, and neat categorization doesn't suit such unruly plants. However, I've tried to deal with weed recipes, weeds for health and so on in separate chapters – though you will find some plants occupying several niches in this book,

and I apologize for any repetition this may cause. The botanical name is included when the plant is first mentioned. Latin names can be daunting, but they do identify a plant precisely, and after a while they begin to make sense – even though they are changed sometimes due to botanists' reclassification.

OLD ENGLISH HERBALISTS

The history of our use of weeds sheds light on what we are missing when we ignore them. Many weeds are mentioned in the pages of old herbals, beginning with the Greeks and Romans.

Henry VIII granted herbalists the right to practise in the 'Quack's Charter', as it became known, though much herbal tradition was inevitably lost during times of upheaval such as the Civil War. There was periodic persecution of witches, such as during the reign of James I, including the famous trial of the Pendle witches in Lancashire in 1612. Many people believed that those who used herbs were in league with the devil.

Several old English herbals are still in print and are worth a look, even though some of their ideas have not survived the test of time. John Gerard and Nicholas Culpeper are two of the herbalists who wrote down their knowledge in order to help people.

John Gerard (1545–1612)

Gerard was a botanist and herbalist, a practical man trained as a barber-surgeon who also looked after gardens for Lord Burleigh. His *Herball or the Generall Historie of Plantes*, first published in 1597, can now be read online, each page reproduced as it is in the original. The book did recycle material and illustrations from earlier writers, but Gerard added much from his own experience and flavoured it with his individual style.

Nicholas Culpeper (1616–1654)

Culpeper was a passionate radical and republican who believed that poor people should have access to medical knowledge. Doctors of the time were fond of quoting Latin and keeping their patients in ignorance, but Culpeper attacked the closed shop of the College of Physicians, growling: 'No man deserves to starve to pay an insolent, insulting physician' – and this is the tone of his writing. Naturally he was most unpopular with physicians because he treated poor people for free, and translated Latin medical texts into English.

Culpeper did his best to instruct people on how to stay healthy, but he was not destined to live to an old age himself. Acting as a surgeon on the battlefield of Newbury during the Civil War, he was wounded in the chest and died of tuberculosis aged thirty-seven.

CONCLUSION

The weeds in this book are a small selection of the many plants at our disposal, and I hope you will consult other sources, both ancient and modern, to add to your enjoyment of the weeds you find. Identification is greatly helped by the excellent photographs you can find on many internet sites.

1 COLONIZATION BY WEEDS

Plants make soil. They create organic material by photosynthesis, a process by which they convert energy from the sun into chemical energy. They manage the mineral content by taking minerals from deeper in the earth, making them available to other plants, and they balance soil pH, the measure of alkalinity/acidity. They do it as a diverse collection of plant species, as part of the natural scheme of things.

This is why bare soil doesn't remain bare: it's not a natural state, in spite of the fact that our ancestors loved to see the ridge and furrow of ploughed land. The Earth's natural cover is a green mantle of vegetation, keeping the soil in good health and holding it from erosion – and much of it is weeds.

WEEDS AND BARE SOIL

Bare soil erodes easily in wind and rain and sun, losing fertility as the mineral content leaches down to the subsoil and the teeming community

Weeds emerging in bare soil.

of microbes and insects diminishes. Heavy rain is beneficial if the soil is covered, but bad news for bare soil. Weed cover is much better than no cover at all.

Healthy soil is a living collection of micro-organisms including insects, worms and fungi that enable plant roots to absorb nutrients. It's an inter-dependent relationship. Bare soil soon forms a dry crust, or in wet seasons a mud bath, in which few of these can live. Years ago I was told by a scientist that to grow food you only need soil to prop up the plants while you feed them with chemicals. Now, more people are aware of the complex reality of plants and their inter-dependence with the soil.

Many soil organisms break down dead plant and animal tissues, thus releasing nutrients in a simpler, soluble form that other plants can use. Some, such as slugs and snails, are pests (although snails are food for some people), and some are organisms that can cause disease, but most are beneficial bugs. It has been said that one square metre of fertile soil can carry as many as a thousand million organisms – but who would volunteer to count them?

Bare soil has no attraction for worms, so they eventually go elsewhere. But earthworms are very important to soil fertility, and if your soil has no worms it's in a bad way; hence the popularity of worm farms. Worms are assistants in the process of soil making. They drag down leaf litter from the surface and also digest it, so developing the structure of the soil. If you are dealing with poor soil, weeds and worms can help you. It's a good idea to imitate the worms and dig in small weeds.

Compacted soil is hard for roots to penetrate and offers nothing to the soil organisms. But plantain (*Plantago species*) colonizes beaten earth, giving shade, food and shelter to what comes next. We'll meet this useful plant again later as part of the rural first-aid kit. This weed, like so many others, went with settlers to the New World: there it appeared on beaten tracks so often that it became known as White Man's Foot. Plantain specializes in hard ground, but grows much bigger in grassland.

Tiny weeds such as scarlet pimpernel (*Anagallis arvensis*) help to cover dry ground. This is a native annual, dying down each year after producing seeds. There is also a blue form, equally attractive, which is found in Spain and other places with plenty of sunshine. The flowers of pimpernel

Broadleaved plantain.

Scarlet pimpernel.

only open in good weather – it's a countryman's barometer – and only from about nine in the morning to three in the afternoon. I had to watch carefully to get a photograph, because when the flowers are closed they are hidden in the leaves.

Another effect in bare soil is that more air gets into the soil, oxidizing the iron sulphide salts, and this turns to sulphuric acid when the rain comes. So acidity is often a symptom of depleted soil, rather than inherent in the land. The remedy is more plants, possibly weeds, to adjust the pH.

Extreme weather, which is becoming more frequent, tends to have a destabilizing effect on our efforts at farming and gardening. Since humans stopped being hunter-gatherers and turned to agriculture we have been disturbing the soil to grow crops, and grazing vegetation hard with domestic animals. The methods of doing so in Europe, on robust soils, worked reasonably well where climates were temperate and rainfall high, but the same methods created dustbowls in parts of North America and Australia where soils are more fragile. We sometimes see dust storms in lowland England when strong winds blow across arable crops before the seeds have a chance to germinate, and the dry soil, with the seeds, is blown away.

Organic food producers try to reach a compromise, to work with nature and try to find ways of working with the soil, including the use of weeds. On our farm we've treated weedy pastures to a haircut, topping the plants and leaving them to return their nutrients to the soil. Sometimes grazing animals will eat hitherto neglected weeds once they have been cut and have dried out, especially nettles.

So it can be seen that we tend to compound our problems by making enemies of weeds. Weeds come to the rescue of bare soils, rejuvenating them in a way that cultivated crops cannot do. Weeds can tolerate conditions that would kill food plants: they thrive in arid conditions and poor fertility, and create a physical barrier to protect the soil from further degradation.

This, of course, is why it's a good idea to think twice before destroying volunteer garden plants. Sometimes soil has to be prepared well in advance for the next crop, but if you have the choice, only clear weeds from the ground immediately before you sow or plant. Consider tolerating annual weeds in between the rows of beans or cabbages, even if they look untidy.

Slashed before they seed, weeds will form a mulch to retain soil moisture, but you have to be vigilant. Some, like chickweed (*Stellaria media*), can re-root given half a chance and a shower of rain. Perennials, once they get a hold, will be a nuisance, and if the annuals drop their seeds you'll have more the following year, or even later in the same year if conditions suit them.

A cover of weeds keeps the soil cooler in summer and warmer in winter, and it encourages the micro-life down there to flourish – but this is not all. Deep-rooted weeds retrieve the lost minerals that are washed down into the subsoil, where shallow-rooted plants such as grass cannot go. These minerals can be used by other plants when the weeds die on the surface.

The Good Weed/Bad Weed

Weeds that come into degraded ground to colonize it are extremely resilient, a fact that should endear them to us. However, their very tenacity makes them aggressive invaders of our flower beds, vegetable plots and farms. Weeds have a good side and a bad side, it has to be admitted, which is why we attack them so ferociously.

An extreme example of a good weed/bad weed in the southern states of Australia is the pretty purple flower, *Echium plantagineum*, now famous world-wide, although it doesn't trouble us in England. This garden flower was introduced into New South Wales in the late nineteenth century by a certain Jane Paterson and was soon known as Paterson's Curse. It quickly established and went running wild over neighbouring paddocks, smothering the pastures and spreading to other states. It's easy to pull out when flowering, but for most of the year it lurks unseen in the pasture grasses.

However, this weed is a wonderful colonizer of bare ground in a drought. In South Australia it has helped to feed drought-stricken cattle and

Spot the vegetable bed.

sheep, keeping them alive when the grass had died. This is how it came to be known as 'Salvation Jane' in that state.

This plant helps the soil further, by being alkaline. Peter Andrews, an Australian weed pioneer, says that he cut and baled a stand of Paterson's Curse, spreading it on the ground on which he grew a broccoli crop. The broccoli heads grew to a kilogram in weight, and the pH of the soil at the end was 9.2, which is well on the alkaline side of neutral, pH 7. Broccoli and the other brassica plants like plenty of lime.

Unfortunately there's another downside to Paterson's Curse: it is toxic to horses and to all non-ruminant animals. Rumination, the complicated digestion process of cattle and sheep, presumably neutralizes the poison.

Then there is the question of honey. The honey from this plant is said to be excellent, but a debate is going on as to whether the honey is toxic too, since it contains pyrrolizidine alkaloids (PA), which can cause liver damage. We will be encountering PA again in other plants. Honey producers say that they blend honey from different sources, and this dilutes any toxic effect to an acceptable level.

The type of plants that will turn up to take over bare ground will vary considerably depending on season, climate and altitude, among other variables, but you can be sure there will be several different species: nature doesn't do monoculture. Biodiversity is a much-used word these days and it is exhibited every day in a weedy field or garden. Some farmers and gardeners try to imitate nature by growing several varieties of plant together.

DISPERSAL SYSTEMS FOR WEEDS

So how do the first volunteer plants get there, sometimes only days after you've laboriously cleared a patch of garden? In any way they can. Many lurk in the soil for years, germinating when conditions suit them. Weed seeds in general will last longer than the seeds of cultivated plants, and some of them are astonishingly long-lived. It's said that seeds recovered from ancient Egyptian tombs have been found to be still viable. On the disturbed soil of bomb sites in wartime Britain, a tall flower called rosebay willow-herb grew where buildings had stood for many years.

Brilliant scarlet poppies (*Papaver orientale*) spring up in cornfields that have not been culti-vated for years previously, as they once did on the battlefields of Europe where the ground was torn up by armies.

Some weeds such as dandelion (*Taraxacum*

Poppies at the edge of a wheat field.

officinale), ragwort (*Senecio jacobea*) and many kinds of thistle will blow in on the wind, travelling considerable distances. They produce seeds with a tiny parachute, a clever dispersal system that ensures you receive your neighbour's thistles just where you don't want them.

I've had nuisance weeds invade our garden, which have come in pots from nurseries, small invaders such as hairy bittercress (*Cardamin hirsuta*), which catapults its seeds far and wide, earning it the name 'flickweed'. Liverwort (*Marchantiophyta*) is a simple plant rather like a moss, which grows in plant pots.

Some weeds are said to have jumped ship in ports, lurking in earth used as ballast. Many common weeds used to travel mixed in with sacks of seed corn, or with seeds of all kinds. The purity of seed samples was not such a priority in the past as it is today.

Birds are responsible for the spread of many plants that have berries, as the seeds are designed to pass through a bird's digestive system unharmed. Other weed seeds similarly pass through the gut of grazing animals, to emerge in manure. If you can compost sheep, pig or cow manure so that it heats up, this should kill most weed seeds.

Seeds with burrs such as burdock, or with hairs such as cleavers, cling to the coats of animals and hitch a ride to pastures new. Weeds such as these are particularly unpopular with sheep farmers because they contaminate wool with plant material that is hard to dislodge. They must irritate the sheep, too.

SOIL IMPROVERS

Weeds on degraded soil will grow even though the minerals have leached out, there is nothing to hold moisture, and the beneficial bugs have decamped elsewhere. If you plant garden seedlings in this hostile medium, they won't thrive – but watch the weeds grow! The first ones are often those with long tap roots such as dock (*Rumex* species) and dandelion, which can reach into the subsoil for sustenance. Some of the nightshades do the same thing.

The pioneers will pave the way for shallower-

Dandelion seed head.

rooted weeds such as chickweed (*Stellaria media*), which will cover the ground so well that it won't dry out. Chickweed will also tend to smother other weeds.

Nettles (*Urtica*) and wild brassicas (*Brassica oleracea*) grow roots that are a mass of fibres, helping to stabilize the soil and acting as host to some of the little creatures therein.

Legumes belong to the family *Fabaceae*, which includes peas and beans, and they are among the most valuable colonizers. There are common legume weeds such as vetch (*Vicia* species); these plants are valuable because they take nitrogen from the air and fix it in the soil, which benefits other plants. They do this by means of bacteria such as *Rhizobium* and related organisms that live

Chickweed.

in nodules on their roots. Nitrogen is often a limiting factor for plant growth, but not all plants can manufacture it for themselves.

Vetches are sometimes grown as animal fodder and can escape as a weed. Lucerne or alfalfa (*Medicago sativa*), a cultivated type, is often grown for feeding to cattle, just as it was by the ancient Greeks and Romans. Lucerne hay is popular for horses. Deep roots, going down sometimes to 40 feet, protect lucerne from dry weather, and it can be cut several times during the grazing season. Legumes are high in protein, and weeds such as vetch are good food for poultry and pigs.

Wild white clover (*Trifolium repens*) with its three, or rarely four, round leaves, also contrib-

utes nitrogen. This is a small ground-hugging plant, a good soil cover once it takes a hold. It's a weed in lawns of course, like many other useful plants, but if you can tolerate a weedy lawn you'll be helping the common blue butterfly and many bumblebees. The white or pinkish flowers can be found between May and October.

Leguminous weeds such as vetches and wild clovers may not be the first colonists to venture on to a bare site, but they are not far behind because they can tolerate poor soil. Encourage them, and if they must go, dig them in, don't pull them out. Cultivated varieties of clover sometimes escape from pastures and invade gardens, but they are also helping to improve soil fertility.

Vetch.

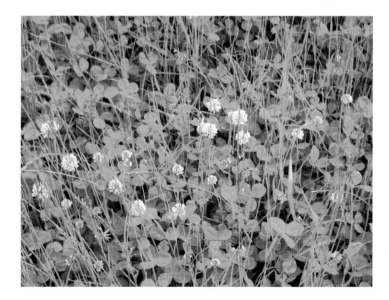

White clover.

WEEDS AS INDICATORS OF SOIL CONDITION

The weeds that invade your space are good indicators of soil condition, although as we've seen, if the soil has been left bare for a long time it won't be as good as it could be. Nettles and fat hen will grow where there is plenty of humus, and you often find them near manure heaps, or in the neglected gardens of empty houses.

Where acidity is high, the *Rumex* family of docks, large and small, will make an appearance, and in gardens, wood sorrel or oxalis (*Oxalis acetosella*). Both plants have been used to give a sharp flavour to food. Country folk in the past, starved of vitamins in long winters, made such delicacies as 'sour dock pudding' using *Rumex acetosa* as soon as the weeds began to grow in spring.

A soil that grows moss is very acid. Mosses are small plants with no flowers or seeds, and are often the first colonizers of ground after trees have been cleared. They like damp situations, but can tolerate dehydration. Heathers hate lime; heather moors have acid soil.

Lichens are the first colonists of really bare sites, for example after a volcanic lava flow, or where all soil has been taken away by a landslide, leaving bare rock. Slowly they gain a foothold, and eventually provide a damp niche for larger plants to exist. Lichens are in fact a combination of algae living amongst the filaments of a fungus in what's called a 'symbiotic relationship'. They're not plants, but they live by photosynthesis; perhaps they are Earth's oldest living things, the start of soil creation.

Alkaline, more 'limy' soils may show a different set of weeds, although many of our weeds are

Oxalis.

Crosswort has a greenish flower.

so hardy that they will grow anywhere. Chick-weed loves lime, and so does goosefoot or fat hen (*Chenopodium album*). Crosswort (*Cruciata lae-vipes*) is a small weed with weak stems that likes to grow on chalk or limestone, so its presence can indicate lime in the soil.

Dry and wet soils will vary with our ever more unpredictable seasons, but aramanth (*Araman-thus*) seems to be a plant that likes dry spots, and mallow (*Malva sylvestris*) may appear after a wet summer and winter.

Salinity is a creeping problem that can hide unnoticed; it is seen on land that was once a colliery or other industrial site. Management should include allowing trees, grass and weeds to soak up the salinity.

Thistles of several species are a painful nuisance, especially when you pick up a handful of thistly hay. The flowers can be eaten by goats, but cattle and sheep give them a wide berth, and in grass paddocks thistles reduce the available grazing. Their seeds, as we have noted, float everywhere. But thistles do have a use: they will colonize degraded soil and fertilize it when they die.

In theory, once the thistles have done their job they will disappear, swamped by the grass. I've found that they rot down into excellent compost if you can cut them or pull them out before they seed. The drawback is that when cut or pulled out, they can speed up the process of setting seed and you can end up with dead plants and

Thistles by the sea.

Dock.

thousands of viable, highly mobile seeds, scattering on the breeze, off to colonize somewhere else.

The degree to which weeds are a nuisance sometimes depends on how long they live. Annual weeds die down each year, but of course if you let them set seed you'll have more of the same the following season. Annuals are only as large as they can grow in one season.

Biennials take two years to grow and reproduce before they die off – for example, plants such as the brassica family that flower in their second year.

Perennials are the ones that can take over if you're not careful, plants that either don't die down in winter, or which survive underground in roots, rhizomes or bulbs, to pop back up again in spring or whenever conditions seem favourable.

Nettle.

2 THE WILDNESS OF WEEDS

The cultivated plants we use today are all derived from wild ones – where else could they have come from? Our forefathers were probably chewing on wild carrots and wild brassicas before they decided to cultivate a patch of ground and put a fence round it. At that point, with some care and a little animal manure, a food plot was made: the first community garden.

Clever folks saved seeds from the biggest and best plants, so that gradually over time the vegetables grew bigger and could feed more people. The other advantage was that the farmers could cut down on food miles because they didn't need to walk so far to find the next meal as when they were gathering wild plants. This gave them the time to invent civilization and develop trades, art and crafts.

However, cultivation led to another change. Over time, the improved plants could no longer survive in the wild outside the fence, or compete with more vigorous, unimproved plants. So the concept of 'weeds' emerged, the plants you didn't want at the time.

The gathering of wild plants persisted for some time after farming came in, and it never quite died out as country folk continued to gather wild food from the hedgerows. We were trained up as gatherers in my childhood, picking watercress, elderberries and mushrooms in their seasons. Foraging is back in favour in the twenty-first century, as a way of getting fresh air and enjoying the pleasure of a hunt. It's a bonus if you can come home with food.

As time went by, the improved vegetables grew larger. But what they gained in size and tenderness due to selection, the

Green aramanth.

vegetable plants lost in hardiness: they needed feeding and watering, protecting from wildlife and competing weeds. The tame plants also eventually lost some flavour, although to our taste this was an advantage on the whole – some wild ancestors of our vegetables are eye-wateringly strong. It's noticeable that the weed varieties of cabbage and the rest are quite strongly flavoured, which makes for an interesting weed salad.

Many of our common vegetables contain oxalic acid and nitrates, too much of which is not good for us. The oxalic acid content of some wild green leaves, such as green aramanth (*Aramanthus*), can be quite high, but is reduced by cooking.

LOSSES IN CULTIVATED FOOD PLANTS

Some people believe that in the last fifty years or so, food plants have lost even more flavour. They've been developed to look pretty, totally unblemished, and even in size, so they can be neatly arranged on supermarket shelves. They have to be sorted and packed and then travel many miles without bruising. Commercial fruit and vegetables need to last for weeks after picking – but taste doesn't come into it: you can't see taste when you are buying food. It's true that less flamboyant specimens, fresh picked from the garden, taste much better than the much travelled ones. Chefs, who depend on taste, have started to take an interest in where their vegetables come from, and many now grow their own.

Even more significant is the loss of nutrients as the plants in captivity grew away from their wild origins. We can't know what went on in past centuries, but it seems that the nutritional value of our cultivated plants has declined since 1950 – studies in Japan and the USA have reached the same conclusion. A US study in 2004 found a decline in six out of thirteen nutrients in a group of fruit and vegetables: protein, calcium, phosphorus, iron, riboflavin and ascorbic acid. The decline in protein was 6 per cent, and top of the range was riboflavin at 38 per cent (vitamin B2, vital to health). Japanese scientists thought the decline in food value was due to environ-

mental factors, soil destruction and high processing methods. However, although this could be partly the result of the processing of our food, some raw foods showed the same trend.

This loss means that wild plants are even more valuable to us in the twenty-first century, because the analysis of so many shows a high nutritional content. Thus weeds can make a valuable addition to our diet, and they're there for the picking, with no need to dig. So why are they so neglected?

WEEDS THAT WENT BACK TO THE WILD

Not all the cultivated plants stayed where they were grown. Over centuries some species escaped and went back to being weeds again, trading social status for freedom (which happens to people, too). They found ingenious ways to get out of confinement. Vigorous plants pushed under fences, climbed over walls, or spread their seeds in a variety of ways. Some seeds parachuted their way up and away on the wind, to start a new life elsewhere. Garden rubbish dumped in the wild has led to the spread of many plants, which then became weeds.

Some plants fell out of fashion as tastes changed, perhaps because people wanted easier options. It became easy to transport vegetables around the country, and even the world: there are few shortages of supermarket greens these days. The unfashionable ones merely jumped the fence and took off on their own, their weed inheritance ensuring survival. The private life of plants is a fascinating one. Some are actually making a comeback in spite of their disadvantages as more people discover the virtues of wild greens.

WEEDS WITH SOME HISTORY OF CULTIVATION

This section comprises a selection of escapees and dropouts; you will find more if you enquire into the history of weeds. The plants that have some history of cultivation are often quite palatable, which is why they were once popular.

Nettle (*Urtica dioica, Urtica urens*)

Up to about a hundred years ago, nettles were grown in glass frames in Scotland to provide a green vegetable in early spring. Before they knew about vitamin C, people felt instinctively that they needed greens; several common weeds had great value in winters when fresh food was scarce. It's almost commonplace now to hear people enthusing about nettles. When they are wilted or cooked they lose their sting, and they are extremely nutritious. When young, nettles are very palatable.

More than this, nettles have many other uses, and I would love to hear from anyone who has tried them. The tough fibrous stems of the taller kinds were spun and woven to make a cloth-like linen for sheets and tablecloths. Nettle cloth was common in the eighteenth century in country houses. Like flax, the stems had to be steeped in water to soften them.

The oily seeds are said to have been used to fuel lamps; also, in a shampoo they help to make the hair glossy. Some spinners and weavers use a soft green nettle dye for wool (*see* the section on plant dyes for more on this).

Herb beers were popular in the nineteenth century, and were sometimes made in an effort to

Nettle seeds.

wean 'the workers' from alcoholic beer, which was a standard household drink for centuries. Mrs Grieve, in her classic book *A Modern Herbal*, tells us that 'the nettle beer made by cottagers is often given to their old folk as a remedy for gouty and rheumatic pains, but apart from this purpose it forms a pleasant drink'. If you like ginger beer, you'll like the nettle equivalent.

Goosefoot, Lamb's Quarters, Fat Hen (*Chenopodium album*)

Some weed plants are known to have been in use as human food since at least the Iron Age, and this is one example of food in prehistory. Several 'bog people' – human remains preserved in peat bogs – have been found. One example I've seen is Tollund Man, who is in the Silkeborg museum in Denmark. He looks like leather, tanned by the acids in the peat. The stomach contents of such bodies have been analysed, and found to contain a wide variety of

Young nettles.

wild seeds and plants, including very often some of the genus *Chenopodium*. Other plant remains have been collected from known Iron Age sites.

The plant is gradually being valued again, having been viewed as a nuisance weed for a long time. It's seen by some as a wild version of spinach. People are planting it, and it's easy to grow in loamy soil, but you'll probably find enough wild goosefoot if you look for it. It usually grows very well near manure or compost heaps where the soil is rich.

The reason it's not a staple food in our times is probably because the seeds are so small – it's a slow job if you want to dry and grind the seeds to make flour; however, it is nutritious. The leaves are easy to use as a green vegetable. Other *Chenopodium* species are also called goosefoot, because of the shape of the leaves. *C. album* – sometimes called lamb's quarters or white goosefoot – and its related species, such as red goosefoot (*Chenopodium rubrum*), are fast growing and common annual weeds. It's a useful green vegetable when the plants are young, and in some countries, including northern India, it is cultivated as a vegetable and a grain crop. However, the plant can be high in nitrates in some circumstances, and in one US study it was found to be toxic to pigs. Quinoa (*Chenopodium quinoa*), a related species, is grown for its seed and is now used in breakfast cereals. Goosefoot is a wild quinoa.

This weed makes a good companion plant as it attracts leaf miners, which might otherwise attack a food crop. 'Leaf miner' refers to the larvae of a range of creatures that bore into leaves: some moths, sawflies, wasps, flies and beetles are leaf miners. They lay their eggs on leaves, and soon the larvae are munching on a wide range of plants. You can see a trail through the leaf when an attack has occurred.

In many places goosefoot is called 'fat hen', supposedly because the seeds are good for fattening poultry.

Goosefoot's cultivated cousin is *C. bonus henricus*, a perennial called Good King Henry, a rather rare vegetable that sometimes appears on market stalls. The shoots are eaten like asparagus, and the leaves can be picked continually through

Goosefoot.

the summer. It looks similar to goosefoot, but the leaves are more heart-shaped and rather less indented.

There is also a 'bad Henry', a poisonous goosefoot (*C. malus henricus*). This one has a smell like tar, so you wouldn't be tempted to eat it, but all the goosefoots should be eaten in moderation, because of the saponins they contain. Rinsing the seeds before use, as is done with quinoa, should get rid of any saponins, which foam in water.

Like many vegetables, the goosefoots contain oxalic acid, and levels can be higher than normal in drought conditions.

Blackberry (*Rubus fruticosus*)

This is a plant that has cultivated cousins, but still flourishes excessively in the wild; it's loved and hated. Blackberry hedges provide food for animals, birds and people, but if allowed to grow unchecked the plant can put out its long tentacles into grassland, and this is a nuisance plant when it's in the middle of a field. It reduces the area of grazing, since cattle give it a wide berth. Blackberry-infested grassland produces prickly hay, unpleasant to handle and no doubt horrible to eat. Foxes form their dens in thickets of blackberries. That's good from a wildlife point of view, but not so good if the fox steals your chickens.

Blackberries in a dry season.

On the other hand, the fruit of the blackberry is one of the best wild foods, delicious raw or cooked, and high in vitamin C and antioxidants. Blackberry bushes can also have a use in stopping erosion on steep banks, as the long roots hold the soil together, and of course the plants discourage grazing animals, which might add to the erosion.

Blackberry hedges can form a useful windbreak both for plants and livestock, but there is always the risk that they will spread. In the berry season birds will be busily spreading the seeds all over the area, and so will foxes and deer. So it's best to be cautious with blackberries.

There's an old superstition that you don't pick blackberries after the first week in October because the Devil will have put his foot on them.

Purslane (*Portulaca oleracea*)

Purslane is a native almost world-wide, and in Tudor times was a salad vegetable. It's a useful ground cover, and has a fresh, cool flavour. Purslane is popular in France and the Mediterranean countries, where several varieties are still in cultivation. You can buy the seeds in Britain, for sowing under glass in early spring – it doesn't like frost.

The stems are reddish and smooth, and the small round leaves quite glossy. I welcomed purslane when I found it volunteering in a bed of onions, where it covered the bare soil without disturbing the crop. The small yellow flowers appear in summer, and open when the sun shines.

This little plant provides plenty of vitamin C and iron, and is also said to be a source of

Purslane.

omega-3 fatty acids, important for health. It's a useful ingredient of salads and soups, and can be steamed as a vegetable.

Sorrel or Sour Dock (*Rumex acetosa*)

This is another plant that has come down in the world. It was cultivated and used in sauces; a green sauce for fish was popular before lemons were easily available in England, because of the sharply acid taste of the leaves.

An elderly Yorkshire aunt told me that when she was a girl, 'sour dock pudding' was popular in spring, before summer vegetables were available. The sorrel leaves were cooked up in a cloth with onion, nettles and oatmeal, and the tradition continues to this day. There is an annual dock pudding competition in a West Yorkshire village, although it seems that there they use bistort (*Persicaria bistorta*) instead of *Rumex* species.

Wild food gatherers use sorrel as a salad ingredient, but you wouldn't need very much of it. In fact, the juice can be used to remove stains from fabric – it is strong stuff.

The cabbage family has several wayward cousins growing wild on cliffs, by the sea, on tips and wasteland. Some of them may have jumped the fence, and foragers often cook them up as a vegetable, weeds such as wild cabbage (*Brassica oleracea*) or wild carrot (*Daucus carota*).

Wild carrot.

WILD PLANTS' CONTRIBUTION TO BIODIVERSITY

We have now realized the value of biodiversity and how it can be eroded: when an animal or plant becomes extinct, its genes are lost forever. Weed plants are a vital source of botanical biodiversity. These humble or even annoying plants represent a vast pool of genes, and we lose them at our peril.

In the section on weeds and wildlife we will look at the many ways in which weeds contribute to the diversity of complete ecosystems, from support for micro-organisms and insects, all the way up the chain to large mammals.

Then there is the potential, as yet undiscovered, of medicinal value in wild plants. As more of them are investigated for their potential use to medicine, their value to us will increase. Research frequently confirms the value of the use of wild plants as 'cottage remedies'. No longer merely dismissed as old wives' tales, in many parts of the world the value of these remedies has been rediscovered.

To take one example, the elderberries from the elder bush (*Sambucus nigra*) are gathered to make a winter cordial (*see* Chapter 9 for details). Elder flowers are used to make a variety of skin-care products: they are fragrant, softening and anti-inflammatory. Elderflower water graced many an Edwardian lady's dressing table, and a cream made from elderflowers and various oils is recommended for sunburn. A tonic wine can be made from the flowers, but sometimes in the fermentation process it develops an unpleasant smell at one stage.

The sheer range of plants, even on the most unpromising land, implies several benefits for the future. Wild plants are not cosseted and fed with artificial fertilizers, and they are not protected from pests and diseases. As we have seen, the hardiness of weed species means they are more sustainable than the cultivated varieties, and this is important.

Wild plants are often more drought tolerant than their more refined relatives, and less susceptible to extremes of temperature. Given the increasing unpredictability of our climate, this is a survival tactic we might need in the future. Weeds can adapt to changing conditions, growing very fast or maturing early to ensure that they can set seed so that descendants will survive. Have you noticed the tiny versions of common weeds that grow, flower and set seed in dry soil? It's all about survival.

Elder bush in flower.

Wild plants are not sterile, but an increasing number of our food plants are hybridized into sterility for commercial use. This is a part of the horticultural and agricultural industries, and people depend on it for a livelihood; it also ensures predictability in the seeds or plants we buy. But it means a loss of biodiversity. For hybrid plants, each year you have to go back to the seed producers or the plant nursery to get another supply. The traditional method of propagation, saving seeds from your vegetables for another year, doesn't work with hybrids.

However, some people are still saving seed from year to year in the garden. There are also companies dealing in 'open pollinated' varieties of plants, which will set seed and allow you to propagate your own.

Groups of plant lovers all over the world, looking to the future, have started seed banks of useful old varieties that might not find favour with supermarkets. They might be tougher, and they could have virtues that are in danger of being lost. One man calls his collection a 'botanical ark'.

It's interesting that some of the companies selling non-hybrid seeds also carry a stock of seeds of the more useful weeds, such as dandelion. Some pasture-seed mixes contain plantain. There are packets of native wild-flower seeds on sale, for people who hope to counter the disappearance of old-fashioned hay meadows where wild flowers thrived. We have a situation where on the one hand there is a war on weeds, while some gardeners are planting them.

You can imagine a potential scene in the future

Yarrow.

when some disease wipes out all our cultivated carrots and the plant breeders have to start again. We can only hope that wild carrot will still be there in the hedgerows, to be tamed once more. The byways of Britain are fringed with verges containing wild weeds such as this one, and long may they survive.

The genetic modification of plants is even further reaching than hybridization, and has many implications, one of which is the legal practice of patenting plant material and issuing licences for its use. But wild plants are unreconstructed, and free from any modification of their genes.

3 WEEDS IN GARDENS

Garden weeds must be one of our most under-used resources. At most times of the year we can find a green salad in our weedy garden, especially in spring. There are so many edible young greens, safe as long as you identify them correctly. They can be mixed in salads, or cooked lightly as green vegetables. Of course, it's safer not to eat large quantities at one time, and it is certainly not wise to eat weeds exclusively.

Some of the salad weeds will be described in more detail in the farm chapter.

PIRATES IN GARDENS

Some garden plants achieve weed status when they appear unexpectedly, invading parts of the garden reserved for other plants. A few of these gatecrashers can be tolerated, others are to

Ivy on an old building.

be avoided. Weeds with the worst potential are probably the creepers and the plants that produce seeds with parachutes, which float in the wind and spread widely.

Several garden plants have a tendency to take over where they are not wanted and have to be managed with care. They can be nuisance weeds, even worse when inherited from previous, neglectful owners of your patch of land.

Ivy (*Hedera helix*)

If ivy creeps into your life, control it. This is a well known, strong climber and creeper, which can make a useful cover for an ugly concrete water tank – in fact it's a good screen in many situations.

Ivy does have other merits: it gives shelter to several species of small bird, which nest among the closely woven stems; and it can keep old houses from damp, absorbing moisture before it gets to the walls (but then it invades the roof gutters and causes problems). It protects buildings from extremes of temperature, and also from atmospheric pollution, so it's tolerated and even encouraged on some historic buildings.

The big drawback with ivy is that it is a strangler: it can overcome almost any other plant, and will eventually kill some trees. There are up to fifteen species of *Hedera*, an attractive plant with shiny, dark green leaves and greenish flowers, which only appear when the plant has climbed high enough to have shoots in the sun. The stems of the plant put out shoots with small discs at the end that hook themselves into the surface of a wall or the bark of a tree. If they get into a crevice or into soil, they grow roots.

In addition to its capacity to smother vegetation, ivy is toxic.

The berries are poisonous to humans but are so bitter that cases of ivy poisoning are rare; however, they are eaten by birds, which is how it can spread. Handling ivy can cause contact dermatitis in people with an allergy to a substance called falcarinol, which is also found in carrots and celery, but not in toxic amounts.

Periwinkle (*Vinca major*)

Periwinkle, with its pretty blue flowers among dark green leaves, is not to be recommended unless you have a large patch of ground in the shade that needs to be covered. I used to tolerate periwinkle because of its reputation: one of the old herbals says of the plant, 'If thou hast the wort with thee, thou shalt be prosperous and ever acceptable.' This sounds like a good idea, but the 'wort' (an old word for plant) has spread and spread, and I still can't be sure of being prosperous, let alone acceptable. It's a persistent weed that is easy to pull out but very hard to eradicate because it can grow from small pieces of stem.

Hedge Bindweed (*Calystegia sepium*)

Their very attractive white or pink flowers may make you forget that the bindweeds are another

Bindweed.

family of stranglers. The thin climbing tendrils have surprising strength: in gardens, bindweed chokes and kills, dragging down plants; in the wild it swamps native vegetation. This is another plant that can grow from tiny pieces of root left in the ground. However, it is edible, and is listed in the recipe chapter of this book.

Ground Elder (*Aegopodium podagraria*)

This troublesome plant was the bane of my life in one garden I worked in, and it is hated by most gardeners. Blame the Romans, who probably introduced it as a vegetable, and possibly blame the medieval gardeners who cultivated it. Ground elder has light green leaves and white flowers, rather like the elder bush, growing on erect stems up to about a metre high. The problem with this weed is the root system: fleshy white rhizomes break into pieces when you dig them out, and each piece then starts a new plant. Ground elder seems to stay close to human habitation, and the leaves can be eaten. It is one of the first green leaves to appear in the spring.

Another name for the plant is goutweed; it was recommended as a remedy for gout and arthritis, applied externally as a warm poultice.

INVADERS TO TOLERATE

Some of the pirate plants are worth managing because they are so useful. This section describes a few of them.

Honesty (*Lunaria annua*)

For an annual plant, honesty carries a lot of clout. Pretty purple or white flowers spring up in unexpected places, followed by the distinctive seedpods that look like silver pennies and often appear in dried flower arrangements. The plant dies down in winter, and the following spring turns up somewhere else, wherever the seeds can germinate. Honesty is also edible, and is one of the plants on food foragers' lists. The flowers are good in salads, but the young leaves are best before the plant flowers, when it's harder to recognize.

The seeds of honesty are used as a mustard substitute, crushed and mixed with water.

Ground elder roots.

Rocket (*Eruca sativa, Brassica eruca*)

Aragula is the plant's name in America, and it is called 'colewort' in the old herbals. It's called rocket because it grows amazingly quickly, flowers and seeds. It can easily become one of your weeds if you let it set seed, but it is easy to pull out. Rocket is a salad plant, so you might tolerate it in beds of other plants. The pale lemon flowers have four petals with a delicate purple vein through them; at night they have a faint perfume. They, too, can be used in salads. Soon the long seedpods appear, each with a beak at the end. You can still keep picking the leaves, but by now they're a deeper green and the stems are tough. This is a useful plant in hot summer weather, when lettuce tends to wilt.

Rocket seedpods burst when ripe and the seeds scatter; they can be harvested just before this happens, or they can be left to self-propagate. The seeds are edible, suspected in medieval times of being an aphrodisiac – but so were many other plants. The more gossipy herbal books tell you that rocket was forbidden in medieval monasteries, but in those days, greens were not really appreciated. Now, things have changed, and we appreciate the value of green vegetables.

Comfrey (*Symphytum officinale*)

Comfrey is a plant surrounded by argument. Some people revere it as a wonderful healing herb (*see* Chapter 7), while others shudder over the 'PA' – pyrrolizidine alkaloid – it contains,

Rocket.

Comfrey.

and are also afraid that it will spread and swamp their garden. Well, we've lived with comfrey for many years, and haven't yet been poisoned or swamped. It's a most useful plant, and I wouldn't be without it for several reasons; but it is hard to eradicate.

Comfrey flowers in late spring, and the leaves can be cut right down four or five times in the growing season, to yield an astonishing amount of material. This plant is common comfrey, a native of the UK and Europe and naturalized in many parts of the world. It grows by old walls in Fountains Abbey, and I wonder whether it is a survival from a medieval herb garden – shades of Brother Cadfael perhaps? I've heard that it used to be grown near the inns where stagecoaches stopped, because it was useful fodder for hard-worked horses. It is certainly persistent, but I

doubt it would survive near a modernized inn with a large car park.

It is quite a pretty garden plant, grown in our case to make a potash fertilizer and a useful healing ointment. Once you've got it, it will stay with you. It likes a shady spot and plenty of animal manure.

When we plant potatoes we usually line the trench with comfrey leaves – and sometimes a stem can put out roots and we end up with a few rogue comfrey plants in the potato bed. The safest way to use it is to make a 'tea' by soaking the leaves in a tub of water, and this is what I use on tomatoes.

Years ago we used to add comfrey to salads. It was popular with vegetarians because it contains vitamin B12, but the leaves are rather prickly, and because of the alkaloid, most people avoid eating it now. Comfrey is now banned for consumer use in the UK, but it makes a useful farm fodder when grass is short.

Borage (*Borago officinalis*)

A plant related to comfrey, borage wanders all over the place as it spreads seed. Bees love it and the nectar makes good honey, so it's tolerated. It breaks down into a good mulch and is useful in compost. (The '*officinalis*' part of a species name given to some herbs indicates a medical use, from the medieval Latin meaning 'of the officina': the storeroom in a monastery where medicines were kept.)

Borage is cultivated commercially for its seeds, which yield an oil called 'starflower oil' because of its star-like blue flowers. The seeds are the richest known plant source of gamma-linolenic acid

Comfrey fertilizer.

Borage.

(GLA), used to treat a variety of ills including rheumatoid arthritis; but hard evidence of its usefulness seems to be scarce so far. It's interesting that a plant may have been used medicinally for generations before scientists can prove that it really does work.

Nasturtium (*Traepaeolum maius*)

Nasturtium is a wonderful ground cover until it starts to wind itself around shrubs and trees; it is often grown to repel pests. I have to keep rescuing shrubs and even apple trees from the clutches of this rampant flower.

The other name for nasturtium is Indian cress. The flowers and leaves are edible and look good in salads, while the large seeds can be used as a substitute for capers. But you need to keep watching that nasturtium doesn't take over. It's said to discourage fruit pests and so we've grown it at the base of fruit trees for years – but how do you measure the effect?

Nasturtium salad.

Nasturtium takeover.

Raspberry (*Rubus* species)

Raspberry bushes send up suckers, underground roots, as a way of making new canes, and they come up in unexpected places. Birds love the berries and spread the seeds.

This is a very good fruit with high levels of fibre and vitamins, especially vitamin C, but the stray canes can be a nuisance. Raspberry roots are quite strong and can only be pulled out by hand when they are small. So keep an eye on your errant raspberries and don't let them take over.

COMPANION WEEDS IN GARDENS

Many gardeners practise companion planting – growing plants together that can help each other and avoiding those that repel. This is not an exact science, so it's sometimes hard to find the evidence, although many of the lists seem to agree.

In your own garden, how can you tell whether good crops have been improved by helpful companions, or grown well as the result of a good season or fertile soil? It would be interesting but difficult to try controlled experiments.

There are several aspects to this idea. The most usual use of companion planting seems to be based on the fact that some plants can repel pests. Given that weeds are usually so healthy, one would expect that some of them might make good companions to cultivated plants.

Possibly the scent of the plant will cause the pest to depart, as insects search for food plants by smell. Alternatively, the companion will act as a trap crop, attract the pest and cause it to leave your crop alone. If it's suitable it will divert the pest, or maybe they will prefer it to your food crop.

Strong-smelling plants such as wild garlic and wild mint can mask the presence of target plants

Raspberry
volunteer
plant.

Nettles in a vegetable bed.

so that insects lay their eggs elsewhere. Bare ground between the rows of plants like cabbages makes it easy for pests to home in on them, but weeds can disrupt their plans and make it hard for them to find the cabbages.

I was taught by my elders that you should plant onions and carrots in alternate rows to confuse the carrot and onion flies, but I never saw a confused fly, although as a child I looked for them. Perhaps they all kept away. Wild carrot (*Daucus carota*), the lacy white flowers of which line country roads in summer, will have the same effect and should help tomatoes and onions.

Nettles are a good example of a companion weed. They are said to repel aphids and are supposed to be good companions for a range of plants including herbs such as marjoram, sage and mint, increasing their essential oil production, and also broccoli and tomatoes.

Borage, the weed herb that romps round my garden as mentioned above, is said to help almost everything, with a beneficial tendency to repel or distract many pests. Borage attracts honeybees, perhaps encouraging them to fertilize the vegetables and fruit as well.

The many brassica weeds should help potatoes, while distracting wireworm.

ALLELOPATHY

Another theory about the effect of companion plants is that of allelopathy, based on the fact that some plants release bio-chemicals into the soil that affect and in many cases inhibit other plants, reducing their growth and reproduction. This term was first used in 1937 and has been the subject of many studies since then. Chemical warfare in plants is not easy to quantify, since the effect could be due to physical crowding rather than an allelopathic effect. An extreme example of this inhibiting factor is a pine plantation, a dark and dismal place with very little life under the trees except for a type of mushroom, the pine mushroom.

Plants can inhibit their neighbours by means of toxins in the leaves; they can pass them on through the roots to other plants in the area, or they can emit poisonous gas.

There can be positive allelopathic effects, however. Wild garlic and other members of the onion family have antibiotic and fungicidal properties that may protect other plants, such as tomatoes, from disease. So has marigold, *Calendula officinalis*.

Marigolds, both *Tagetes* and *Calendula*, are very popular companion plants. My market gardener uncle grew *Calendula* right though his vegetable beds. Uncle Fred loved the colours and believed that marigolds killed pests and helped most plants. It is now thought that they produce a chemical pesticide that lasts in the soil even when they have gone. However, they do seem to attract snails, and they certainly invade different parts of the garden.

This garden invader has also been a much-loved and used herb since ancient times. The brilliant orange and yellow flowers persist for months. Marigold ointment is very soothing (*see* the 'Weeds for Health' chapter for details). I've sometimes added marigold petals to salads. The golden petals can be used to colour butter and cheese, an old method that is still useful for a home dairy.

Calendula marigold.

WEED MULCHES

Another type of allelopathic effect has been suggested: it has been observed that plants won't grow in their own residues. This principle can be used to kill weeds, by slashing them and piling them on the ground. They will inhibit further growth of the weed and allow other plants to grow.

In fact, weed mulches can have several benefits. The garden looks much tidier if you remove weeds and pile them in a heap, and this can eventually make good compost. But if they are left spread on the ground, they will conserve moisture. As they wilt and then decay, minerals will be released on the surface of the soil, where they are needed. Worms will come up and drag the vegetable matter down into the soil, creating more humus.

The only drawback with weed mulch used in this way is that in wet conditions, some weeds such as chickweed will revive and start to grow again. Chickweed can easily be too much of a good thing.

Another way to use a weed mat is to bury it. After the weeds have wilted, dig them into the ground, turning over the soil to bury them, or dig a trench and fill it with weeds.

Purslane seedling.

Purslane (*Portulaca oleracea*), Pigweed

This low-growing plant makes a very good living mulch, conserving moisture and keeping out other weeds. It's a succulent with small, dark green leaves, and often red stems. It's possible that you have pulled out this plant when weeding, without really noticing it. But purslane or pigweed has an interesting history, as previously mentioned. There are cultivated varieties grown as ornamental ground covers; I last saw this 'weed' in a rooftop garden in Singapore, where it was threatening to take over. It has long been grown as a vegetable in Holland and France.

DON'T DUMP GARDEN WEEDS

Local councils frequently ask us not to dump weeds in the countryside or on roadsides, and when we're considering all their benefits, this might seem unnecessary. But garden weeds can soon suppress native plants and change the whole ecosystem, ultimately affecting the resident insects, birds and animals. Blackberries and ivy are obvious invaders, but there are many more. We do have a responsibility to keep pirate plants under control.

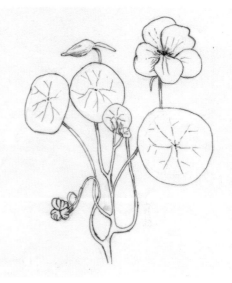

Nasturtium.

4 WEEDS ON SMALL FARMS

Monoculture is common on farms for commercial crops as it simplifies operations. Weeds are banned, and grass is treated very much as a crop, often rotated every few years with vegetables or grain. Even grassland may be confined to one species, and many grass fields are covered in fence-to-fence ryegrass. Commercial ryegrass grows fast and keeps going – but there must be many herds of bored cows, because grazing animals much prefer a mixture of plants in their diet. Who wouldn't? There are grassland weeds that are of benefit, but are not likely to take over as the invasive species do. These can be useful plants in a pasture.

Permanent grass pastures that are never ploughed used to be the norm and still exist in some places, particularly in the hills, in the west of Britain and on land unsuitable for ploughing. Traditionally some grass fields would be mown for hay every year, followed by grazing when the grass had grown again. Old pastures and hay meadows are a haven for many species of wildlife. We'll look at their value in the wildlife section of the book.

On our family's small farm, Lime Tree Farm, we milked cows and kept pigs for years. My brother Peter and his wife Irene now run the farm, and have gradually changed the way things are managed to a more conservation-based policy. They were partly helped by a government stewardship scheme, which encouraged landowners to conserve and restore wildlife habitats and encourage educational access. Peter and Irene are now quite well known for their efforts in creating a haven for wildlife. People, too, can find peace and can gain greater understanding of the natural world, camping there to attend various educational events.

Lime Tree Farm is now a place where wild plants flourish, as well as providing a diversity of habitats for animals, birds and insects. The grass is grazed by sheep and sometimes by young cattle. Some hay is made late in the season, to allow meadow flowers to blossom and set seed.

Not every farmer can convert in this way, but the Lime Tree experience shows what can be done in small ways by farmers who want to encourage and conserve wildlife alongside normal farming activities. Every little helps. As we will see in the wildlife section, the edges of fields, ponds and streams, and small areas of wetland or woodland can co-exist with farming enterprises to support butterflies, birds, bees and many other creatures. Weeds are a vital part of the equation, and it is heartening to see how many arable fields on commercial farms now have a border of weeds. Local councils in many places are cutting back on slashing grass, whether from budget constraints or for environmental reasons.

In walks round the countryside it is possible to see that weeds are not being suppressed as rigorously as they used to be. Arable farms may exhibit clean stands of cereals or beans – perhaps with a few poppies – but round the edges there are weeds and more weeds, unrepentant, in many a farm in the north and west of Britain.

WEEDS FOR SHELTER AND SHADE

Natural hedges are formed by shrubby weeds, often those such as hawthorn that make good stock barriers. Hedges on many farms have been removed as fields were enlarged to take modern machinery; others gave way to urban develop-

Hedge with wildlife field margin.

ment. The Hedgerow Regulations 1997 were formed to protect exceptionally species-rich hedgerows, some of which are of great age.

The older hedges on our farm are about 200 years old, dating from the land enclosure acts; most field hedges in England are no older than this, but there are a few ancient ones. Our hedges used to be trimmed every autumn, but now they are allowed to grow, and they provide much more shelter.

If you want to work out the age of a hedge, try Hooper's Rule. In his book *Hedges*, published in 1974, Dr Hooper suggests that the age of a hedge equals the number of woody species counted in a 30-yard stretch, multiplied by 110 years. This is not infallible, but in general the more species in a hedge, the older it is.

An exception to this is a newly planted hedge, which will usually have a good mix of species. Hedges are still are being planted by conserva-

tion-minded landholders because of their value. Hedge species harbour smaller weeds, and the weeds provide shade, shelter and food for a large number of different creatures – although tidy farmers complain about hedgerow weeds, and also bemoan the fact that hedges take more management than fences.

A good hedge and its weeds has several advantages to the farmer. It provides shelter and shade for livestock, which is especially valuable in extreme weather conditions. The shelter extends to the grass on which the stock depend. One farmer I met had been able to carry more grazing animals on his farm after planting hedges and trees, even though by doing so he had decreased the amount of land available for grazing.

Patches of woodland, even small ones, can alter the microclimate of a farm and provide stock havens, and places where weeds can live without annoying people.

Woodland shelter for poultry.

Cattle eating cut comfrey on our farm in Australia.

Self-sown trees can appear as giant 'weeds' on corners of land left to their own devices. Small plantations grown for sale will shelter farm animals.

FARM WEEDS AS STOCK FEED

There are weeds on farms that can provide food for many types of livestock. Comfrey, mentioned in the garden section, can be invasive, but it's a good food for grazing animals. A stand of weeds might be controlled by cutting, drying and making as hay for stock feed.

Mallow (*Malva parviflora, M. neglecta* and other *Malva* species)

Mallow is often called marshmallow. True marshmallow (*Althaea officinalis*) is a related plant used in medicine, and traditionally to make marshmallow sweets, although modern recipes use gelatine.

Mallow is eaten by sheep and cattle, usually with no problems. However, cases of poisoning have occurred where animals, particularly lambs, have eaten mallow and nothing else, which might be the case if they were confined to a small area. They can develop the condition called 'staggers', and spend much time lying down. There is no cure, but animals will recover once they have access to grass.

Plantain (*Plantago major, P. lanceolata*)

The plantain weed is a widespread green leaf, common where land has been cultivated. The leaves are either long and narrow (ribwort) or round (broadleaved plantain). The plant forms a rosette at the base, with long, thin, leafless stems bearing brownish flowers.

Plantain seems to have been associated with cultivation from earliest times, and those who study pollen distribution use it as an indicator of prehistoric farming at a given site.

The benefits of pasture 'weeds' such as plantain are now well known. Plantain is so common you

Mallow.

will probably find it in any grass paddock, though it's a leaf that people hate to see in lawns. It's now added as a forage plant to some permanent pasture seed mixtures, giving diversity to the diet for cattle and sheep and supplying protein. Plantain leaf is said to contain over 23 per cent crude protein; the ribbed leaves make it unmistakeable, in either its wide-leaved or narrow-leaved form.

One day I observed a patch of plantain in a field of fresh new grass, before the cattle were moved in. When I checked later they had eaten the lot, so they obviously knew the value of the plant. Plantain seed heads provide food for various small birds, so if the livestock don't eat the plant the birds will benefit.

As we've noted earlier, plantain is a drought-tolerant plant with a high protein and mineral content, since it has a long tap root, with which it brings up minerals from the lower reaches of the soil. Many of our weeds have the same properties.

Yarrow (*Achillea millefolium*)

Yarrow is another beneficial pasture weed, one that used to be sown in grass mixtures. It's often there in pastures, but the feathery leaves are not conspicuous. Yarrow is only really noticeable in early summer, when the whitish or pink flowers appear, growing in a flat-topped cluster at the top of the stem. Some nurseries sell the pink form as

Yarrow.

This is another weed with a good side and a bad side. It's a nuisance in grain-growing districts because green material is not wanted in harvested grain. Like the other plants with downy seeds, sow thistle spreads easily, since its seeds have tiny parachutes and are blown by the wind. The seeds catch in hedges and on fences. It's an annual plant and the seeds can survive for a year on the surface, longer in the soil. It can also invade grassland in a wet season.

On small farms, however, sow thistle can be useful, producing a lot of bulk and appreciated as food by pigs – of course – and also by cattle. Some of our Australian cows are very fond of it. Cows and calves eat the flowers and the tender top third or so of the stem; it can also be fed to poultry. To prevent a serious invasion, use it before it sets seed.

an ornamental plant. In the garden it's a good companion plant and a useful addition to compost.

On the farm, yarrow is valued for its drought resistance and its deep roots. This is another plant that brings minerals up to the surface, and so in pastures it should help to prevent mineral deficiencies in livestock. I haven't observed animals eating yarrow, but when it dies the minerals will be there for the grasses. No doubt it will be eaten in a drought.

Drought-resistant plants such as yarrow will also help to combat soil erosion, providing a green cover when grasses have died down.

Sow Thistle (*Sonchus oleraceus*)

Sow thistle (also called milk thistle) sometimes appears at the edges of paddocks; it is a soft thistle with a small yellow flower and a milky sap in the hollow stem. It's not a true thistle, but like the thistle family it has a long tap root and a high mineral content. We have both this form and the more prickly type (S. *asper*).

Chickweed (*Stellaria media*)

This little plant has made itself at home in most parts of the world. It has small, light-green leaves, only 1cm long, that grow on weak, sprawling stems. The tiny flowers are like white stars. At night the leaves fold over to protect the new shoots. Chickweed likes shady and moist conditions. It makes a good 'living mulch' round trees and tall plants such as sweetcorn, but smaller plants can be swamped because of its sheer volume. You don't find it in pastures very often because grazing animals eat it whenever it's within reach.

Sow thistle.

Aramanth.

As the name suggests, chickweed makes a good green food for poultry, and also for pigs. It's useful as a feed to animals that have to be confined to a pen. A patch of chickweed can be cut several times in a growing season. It can be added to salads, or lightly steamed as a vegetable.

Green Aramanth (*Aramanthus viridis*)

Now hailed as a 'super green', aramanth is a nutritious weed also known as pigweed.

Lemon Balm, Bee Balm (*Melissa officinalis*)

This fragrant plant is a perennial related to mint, often seen in gardens but

also sometimes used by organic farmers in grassland seed mixtures. Some people believe it is good

Lemon balm.

for dairy cows. The leaves have a sweet lemony scent and taste, and the white flowers produce a great deal of nectar for bees. Like its relative mint, this is another plant that can spread vigorously and may need to be kept in check.

Insects are kept away when the skin is rubbed with lemon balm leaves. As a herb, this plant has a wide variety of uses. It has a calming effect, and is said to improve mental performance. Lemon balm tea, made by steeping fresh leaves in boiling water, has a pleasant flavour and is well worth a try.

WEEDS FOR ANIMAL BEDDING

Bracken (*Pteridium*) is a common weed, especially on upland farms, and is difficult to eradicate. It's a large, coarse fern, probably the most common fern in the world. It can make useful bedding for animals in winter if it's cut, dried and stored during the summer. The used bedding makes a good mulch.

Fields with rushes, tussock grass and other coarse grasses can get worse with time, as grazing animals avoid the coarser plants and big clumps are formed. Such fields will be improved by cutting, and the resulting rough dried grass will make good bedding. The animals may eat some of it, but that won't matter. Next spring the more nutritious grasses should have a better chance of growing, so the area will produce more grazing.

IMPROVING GRAZING PASTURES

Dry seasons tend to degrade pastures; for example, cattle tend to favour certain areas for lying up and chewing the cud, and in dry times these areas may lose all their vegetation, allowing weeds to creep in and recolonize them. In wet seasons, weeds such as docks seem to spread extensively in boggy areas, as cattle and sheep churn up the surface of the ground until only weeds can survive there. Thistles like rainy weather and can grow at an alarming rate.

All this means that grass pastures need a certain amount of management to be at their best.

Frequent light grazing is nearly always better than allowing stock to bite down grass to the roots.

Young grain plants make good grazing, and can usually crowd out weeds. They are also used as a green manure mixture, and are turned into the soil when half grown.

FARM MULCHES

Slashing weeds and leaving them on the surface as a mulch is an excellent practice for weedy grass fields, if you can get to the weeds before they set seed. Cattle will often eat wilted weeds such as nettles, but if they don't, the plants will still be adding their nutritional content to the surface.

There are several machines specifically designed to cut paddocks to mulch them. The mulcher is hitched to the tractor and has several height settings. Just as in gardens, mulching is a good technique for weed control on farms.

MORE FARM WEEDS

Tussock Grasses

Tussock grasses are weeds of permanent pasture. There are various species that grow into mounded clumps (for example *Poa* species). Some are hated, but others have uses: for example, they often have long roots that can stabilize soil and help heavy rain to penetrate. Tussocks provide shelter and food for many insects, small animals and birds, and shelter for calves and lambs in paddocks. Mats, baskets and bags can be woven from their fibrous stems.

Some of them, being drought resistant, are used in ornamental gardens. However, the serrated tussock (*Nassella trichotoma*), a feathery-looking plant, is a seriously invasive weed from South America, which is spreading round the world. It can invade any type of land, but it has no feed value and stock don't like it. The seeds can contaminate hay and grain, and can be spread by farm machinery from place to place. It's hard to eradicate, so keep a watch for it – there are small pockets of it in Britain.

Dandelion (*Taraxacum officinale*)

This weed is too bitter for most animals to eat, but it is quite common in permanent grass paddocks on farms. The name is derived from 'lion's tooth' (French *dent de lion*) because of the serrated leaves. The bright yellow, single flower grows on a hollow stem that emerges from a rosette of leaves in spring and summer. The seeds are blown off on a parachute.

This is another plant listed in the herbals, as an important diuretic and detoxifying herb. It is supposed to help weight loss by metabolizing fats.

Dandelion is not to be confused with the various cat's ears species, which have thin, hairy stems (*see* below). The true dandelion has a thick stem with milky juice.

You wouldn't want too many dandelion seeds blowing about the farm, but the plant is useful before it sets seed as the yellow flowers are attractive to bees.

Cat's Ear or Flatweed (*Hypochoeris radicata*)

This plant is often mistaken for dandelion, but it is skinnier and tougher, and has several flower stalks springing from one base. It is very common in wet areas and is usually regarded as a nuisance in pastures as well as in lawns. Its other name is flatweed because the rosette of leaves lies flat to the ground. The seeds spread by parachute, like those of dandelion.

Cat's ear is eaten by livestock and can be used as a herbal remedy instead of dandelion; it is said to be similar in action, but milder. In some cultures the plant is valued as a vegetable.

Cat's ear.

Wild rose.

Wild Rose (*Rosa rubiginosa, Rose canina*)

Sweet briar and dog rose are both seen on farm-land. The dog rose has flower stalks without prickles and very pointed leaflets. Wild roses are undesirable on farms because grazing animals can be scratched, and also, the prickly patches form shelter for foxes and rabbits.

However, sweet briar has some favourable characteristics. The scarlet berries, called rose hips, feed birds, and the flowers yield pollen for bees. (*See* Chapter 9 for rose-hip jelly.)

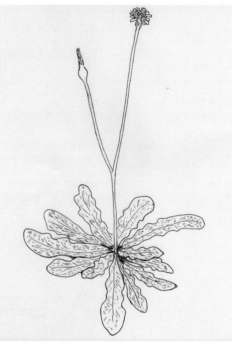

Cat's ear.

POISONOUS WEEDS: A CHECKLIST

The following plants have all been mentioned in various sections of this book.

Weeds to avoid in animal food include ragwort (*Senecio jacobea*). Sheep can tolerate this plant in small doses, and in fact can control it by eating the young plants, but it is toxic to cattle and horses. I don't think they would eat ragwort unless there was nothing else – in my experience they ignore it.

St John's Wort (*Hypericum*): This plant can cause photosensitization, a condition that in cattle causes the skin on any white patches of their coat to blister and peel away.

Foxglove (*Digitalis*): Would be poisonous in large amounts. The tall spikes of bell-shaped flowers grow in hedges and walls on farmland, usually without causing problems.

Elder (*Sambucus nigra*): A hedgerow shrub or small tree. Its leaves and branches can be toxic to grazing animals, and so can the wilted leaves of fruit trees. This means that pruned branches from such trees should be kept well away from animals, especially goats, which like to nibble something new.

Sneezewort (*Achillea ptarmica*): Related to yarrow, but this plant is also poisonous to grazing animals.

Ragwort.

Foxglove, beautiful but poisonous.

5 WEEDS FOR WILDLIFE

Lime Tree Farm, my family's small patch of Yorkshire, was mentioned in the section on small farms. The farm is now partly a nature reserve and a place where people go to study various forms of wildlife because of the diverse habitat the farm provides. Ornithologists ring birds frequently and compile records, which are sent to the Royal Society for the Protection of Birds (RSPB). This, of course, contributes to the national database of bird populations. Ecologists conduct various studies, butterfly and moth experts visit,

and schools undertake projects, while among the wild plants, the wild creatures get on with their business.

Diversity on these 16 hectares is increased by the fact that the land sits between moorland, from which it was enclosed two hundred years ago, and farmland at a lower level. Some fields have drystone wall boundaries, others have hedges; there are meadows, woodland, ponds and a stream or beck as we call it, running through a little valley with steep sides where orchids grow,

Pied flycatcher in woodland.

Bumblebee on vetch.

called in these parts a gill. For the last thirty years or so, plenty of weeds have come back to add to the diversity. Every time I visit there is more wildlife, from minute pond creatures to the occasional deer.

As we've already noted in passing, suppressing weeds, as good farmers need to do, removes habitat for many of the wild creatures that enrich our environment and have a beneficial effect on gardens and farms. The wildlife around us fits into various niches in ecosystems, but when links in the complicated chain of life are missing, the system falters. Wild plants are a vital link.

Even a small patch of flowering weeds provides nectar and pollen for insects. Many of us have a natural aversion to insects, but among them are beneficial pollinators. Bumblebees are suffering from a lack of suitable habitat and are declining in numbers. Insects are a vital support in ecosystems, feeding creatures higher up the chain: birds and mammals.

GRASSLAND HABITAT AND ITS FLORA AND FAUNA

Grass left uncut will grow long and eventually produce seeds. Longer grass and its seeds will allow insects, amphibians and small mammals to pursue their lifestyles in peace, while giving space and shelter for other plants to flower.

Grassland Flora

Self-heal (*Prunella vulgaris*) is one such meadow plant; it was once a valued medical herb because of its astringency, and was used to treat burns,

Meadow cranesbill.

sores and bruises. In Chinese medicine self-heal is used internally as a liver treatment. Meadow cranesbill (*Geranium pratense*) is a beautiful wild flower, sometimes grown in gardens and most attractive to bees and butterflies. This is an important flower meadow species.

Bird's-foot trefoil (*Lotus corniculatus*) is often lurking in grass, the bright yellow flowers visible in summer. This weed is a legume, fixing nitrogen from the air. It is a food plant for the larvae of several moths and butterflies, particularly the common blue. The caterpillar is small and green with yellow stripes.

Red clover (*Trifolium pratense*) and white clover (*Trifolium repens*) are valuable nectar and pollen plants, as well as food for grazing animals. Clovers are legumes, and because they fix nitro-gen, their pollen is high in protein. Bumblebees in particular need plenty of protein, and clover is important to them.

These and many other weeds are very often denied the chance of flowering because they are cut down by mower blades. Silage – grass preserved by fermentation – is often cut in May, and there may be two more cuts during the growing season. This is naturally to the detriment of wildlife. Hay, on the other hand, is grass that is cut, dried and baled for winter fodder on many farms, and this is usually mown in June or early July while the protein in the grass is high. Some farmers make hay as a commercial crop to sell. This is more helpful to wild plants because meadows that are cut for hay later in the season means that wild flowers are able to bloom

Red clover.

and then set seed. Corners and edges of fields can be left uncut, leaving wildlife habitats among the weeds, and this is becoming more common now.

Grassland Birds

A late cut also helps birds. If meadows are cut for hay at the end of July, ground nesting birds such as skylark, lapwing and curlew can hatch their chicks in safety. Once common, these birds are rarer now because of their shrinking habitat. The skylark is a 'red list' species: this is an international list of threatened species. The small brown bird is not easy to spot on the ground, but is immediately identified by its joyous song as it ascends higher and higher into the sky.

Some birds feed on the plants or on the creatures that feed on the plants, and others weave their nests from dried grasses.

Grassland Mammals

There are mammals lurking in the long weedy grass areas too: hares, field mice, voles, stoats, foxes and hedgehogs. 'Field mouse' is a term used for a range of mice, but the true field mouse is the long-tailed field mouse or wood mouse, a creature with large eyes and ears and about 10cm (4in) long. This mouse eats anything it can lay its paws on, including seeds and berries, and is eaten in turn by a range of predators including owls – thus a good habitat for mice also helps the owl population.

If you are trying to make a living from livestock farming, of course you need to maximize the amount of grass you grow by reseeding with improved grasses specially bred for production, and by applying fertilizers. But the resulting vigorous grass growth, even with organic fertilizers, inevitably suppresses weeds and reduces the food supply for the wild creatures living there.

Meadow Flowers

Meadow flowers include lady's bedstraw (*Galium verum*), bird's-foot trefoil and red campion (*Silene dioica*).

Ragged robin (*Lychnis flos-cuculi*) grows in damp areas and provides nectar for many butterflies and bees. Meadow cranesbill (*Geranium pratense*) is often seen on roadsides and hedge banks, often on limy soils. This is one of several cranesbills; the seeds are carried on stalks that curve like a crane's bill. Spotted orchid (*Dactylorhiza fuchsii*) lurks in the damp grass.

During the spring, marsh marigold (*Caltha palustris*) gleams in damp and partly shaded areas in the gill, on a part of the farm that has never been fertilized or 'improved'. Moths, butterflies and many other insects are attracted by the flowers. Annual meadow grass (*Poa annua*), not a showy plant, is host to the meadow brown, ringlet and wall butterflies.

Bees

Harebells (*Campanula rotundifolia*), called bluebells in Scotland, are delicate little bells of light blue, and we find them in upland pastures, usually in the edges of fields or in wall bottoms. Harebell carpenter bees, more common in the south of England, are small, solitary bees that are seen hovering around harebells. They sometimes sleep in the bells, and may mate in them. These tiny black bees are seen in groups near harebells at times; they nest in small crevices and holes in wooden fences and sheds.

Red campion.

Spotted orchid.

Bees in hives are not strictly wildlife, although feral honeybees living in trees are quite common. Bees give us one of our most ancient foods, honey, and several other products such as beeswax. We also depend on bees for the pollination of many of our food plants – some sources suggest that up to 60 per cent of plants rely on bees for reproduction.

The black bee (*Apis mellifera mellifera*) has been the dominant honeybee since the last Ice Age, and is well adapted to our UK climate. But it almost became extinct through the attacks of an internal parasite called Isle of Wight disease. However, these hardy little bees have survived up to now, and their genes are present in many of our honeybees. There is a campaign to help the black bee by creating breeding centres and encouraging beekeepers to look after it.

The commercial honeybee today is often the Italian bee, a small European bee with yellow bands on the abdomen. Bees are used to polli-nate crops such as oilseed rape and peppers. Some large-scale bee-keeping operations are responsible for the pollination of commercial crops. Our native flowering plants are their favourites, and many of them are weeds, so weeds support many beehives.

Honeybees need weeds.

Bumblebee on thistle flower.

Bumblebees are important for the pollination of tomatoes and many other food plants. They, too, have been under stress, and the short-haired bumblebee is now extinct in the UK. The Bumblebee Conservation Trust (BBCT), founded by Professor Dave Goulson, is committed to disseminating information about them. At Lime Tree, several species of bumblebee buzz round the flowers on a warm day.

Flower meadows are vital to bumblebees, and they also need places to nest in, often holes or empty mice nests. Mice eat bumblebee nests, so control of mice helps the bees.

For the last few years, bee populations have declined all over the world. There are several threats to their welfare, including poison in the form of farm chemicals and garden sprays. Extreme weather conditions such as excessive rain and wind are becoming more common, and in a drought, plants produce little if any nectar and

pollen, on which bees depend for survival. Then there are various bee diseases, pests and parasites that they have to contend with.

Add to all these hazards a decline in the weed population, and you start to feel sorry for the bees. So here's another, really good excuse for a weedy garden: 'I'm growing flowers for the bees.' Dandelions are favourites because they flower in early spring, before the main blossom time has started. Year-round flowers are what the bees want, and often, the gaps are filled by weeds.

Weeds have another virtue from the bees' point of view: they have not been bred up to produce lots of frilly petals, like some showy garden flowers, and layers of petals are a nuisance to bees, as they hamper their efforts to get to the pollen and nectar. Some modern sterile garden flowers in fact have no pollen and nectar, so you can see why weeds are important.

Too many petals hamper bees.

Many of the plants previously mentioned are 'bee-friendly', and a lot of them attract moths and butterflies as well. Bees seem to like blue or purple-coloured flowers in particular. Comfrey and borage, daisy (*Bellis perennis*), chickweed, flatweed, nettle and thistle flowers all provide food for bees.

The 'Good Bugs'

Insects make up over 70 per cent of biodiversity, but many are still not documented. There is growing interest in the biological control of pests, with some pest predators available in commercial quantities. But many useful insects are killed by the sprays that are designed to destroy the very pests that they can remove.

In gardens and small farms it pays to recognize the 'good bugs', and to encourage them, first of all by not using sprays. They can be helped by allowing weed cover to grow and flower, giving them shelter and food. The daisy family, wild carrot and many other weeds can host them.

It's interesting to identify some of these beneficial insects. Ladybirds are easy to spot, and may be yellow, orange or red, with black spots on their wing covers. They are predatory beetles and feed on aphids, mites, moth eggs, scale insects and mealy bugs. They are good at picking off aphids on roses, given time, and are often supported by weeds. Most ladybirds are beneficial, though some species do eat our food plants.

Parasitic wasps will also control aphids, and some lay their eggs in moth eggs. Hoverflies are distinctive with their black and yellow abdomen; they need pollen and nectar from flowers, but their larvae eat aphids and mites.

Encouraging insects by allowing your weeds to thrive will also help to support bird life. Many birds live on the insects that are attracted to weed species, and can reduce the population of pest species. Other birds are seed eaters and tuck into weed and grass seeds.

Thus the grassland habitat is vital to many species.

HEDGEROW AND WOODLAND HABITAT

A study by the British Trust for Ornithology with Oxford University showed that hedgerow weeds play a very important role in attracting and feeding birds. Studies on organic farms showed that where sprays were not used and weeds were allowed to grow on the margins of the fields and in hedgerows, there was a rich variety of berries and seeds for birds (published in the Royal Society Journal *Biology Letters*, August 2005).

Hedges form wildlife corridors, allowing safe movement from one patch of shelter to another, and they have become more important as the areas of woodland have decreased. Birds nest in hedges, finding nest materials, food and safety there. Good hedges include trees, shrubs and a ground cover of weeds and grasses, offering nesting sites for a variety of birds including wood

pigeon, magpie, mistlethrush, little and tawny owls and the greater spotted woodpecker.

Plants and Wildlife

Hawthorn (*Crataegus monogyna*) is one of the most valuable hedgerow plants. It produces fragrant May blossom with nectar and pollen, said to support more than 300 insects. Moth caterpillars feed on the hawthorn leaves, and dormice eat the flowers. Later, the red berries (haws) are important food for migrating birds such as redwings. The redwing is a small thrush, seen mainly in winter and so named because the underside of the wings is red. It breeds in northern countries as far south as the north of Scotland, and flies south for the winter. Hawthorn gives excellent shelter to many nesting birds and small mammals.

Shrubs such as hawthorn give protection and also food to the tree sparrow, bullfinch, wren, chiffchaff and many more. Partridge and pheasant nest under hedges, and willow warbler, yellowhammer and robin make their nests in their foliage. Hedges close to ditches shelter frogs, toads and newts and make good cover for hibernation. Reptiles, adders and grass snakes like the

An old hawthorn.

Hazel.

bottoms of hedges for cover, and they dine on other inhabitants such as mice and shrews.

Hazel (*Corylus avellana*) is common in older hedges. This is the small tree that produces male catkins in early spring before the leaves appear, making us feel that winter is over. The female catkins are small, but you can spot the bright red tips. Hazel nuts provide food for both red and grey squirrels, mice and nut-eating birds such as woodpeckers – and humans.

The pliant stems of hazel have a variety of uses: wattle fences and wall supports (as in wattle and daub), basket making and coracle boat construction. Some plantations of hazel are coppiced – cut down to ground level and left to shoot again – and can be harvested every few years.

Ivy (*Hedera helix*), previously mentioned as a nuisance weed in the garden, is good for wildlife, sheltering several species of small bird and pro-viding hibernation places for insects. The flowers appear in autumn when summer flowers have gone, providing nectar for pollinating insects when other food is scarce. The ivy bee, originating in Europe but now present in Britain, lives on ivy. In winter, ivy berries support blackbirds and thrushes in the hungry gap at the end of winter, when other berries have been eaten.

Woodland Mammals

The common dormouse is also called the hazel dormouse. This little creature with large dark eyes is seldom seen; it is nocturnal and spends most of its time in the branches of trees and shrubs. In addition, the dormouse hibernates for up to six months in winter, in a nest under a pile of leaves or other protection. Even in summer if the weather is cold and wet, the dormouse goes to sleep. Hazelnuts fatten it up for hibernation, though it will eat other nuts and berries and small insects.

The dormouse has friends: the People's Trust for Endangered Species (PTES) is currently introducing the species to suitable locations in Yorkshire, in a bid to rescue it from extinction (*Yorkshire Post* 24 June 2016). Lime Tree was apparently considered a dormouse haven, but it doesn't have enough hazels to support a colony.

The red squirrel is still being displaced by the introduced North American grey squirrel in Britain, although efforts are being made to provide habitat where the reds can compete on equal terms with the greys. Red squirrels prefer conifer woodland, so management of this type of forest is being considered with red squirrels in mind (for example the Kielder Forest Project in Northumberland).

Woodland Flowers

Sweet violet (*Viola odorata*) has a delightful fragrance, but the small white flowers are often hidden in the shady margins of woodland. Violet leaves and flowers are edible and can be added to salads, while herbalists value wild violet species as a support to the immune system and a detoxifying agent for the body.

A small patch of our woodland, sitting between meadows, provides shade for several plants including bluebells (*Hyacinthoides non-scripta*), probably England's favourite flower. Bluebells are protected by laws which make it an offence to dig up or sell the bulbs. These pretty, scented wild flowers look like a blue mist under the trees and are said to indicate the site of ancient woodland. They flower in late spring and are much appreciated by bumblebees. Although they are not used for honey production because they don't store much honey, bumblebees are important pollinators.

Dog's mercury (*Mercurialis perennis*), like the bluebell, indicates the site of ancient woodland, but it spreads to hedgerows and can be found in the cracks of limestone pavements. This plant is on the poisons list. It flowers in early spring, the pollen blown by the wind.

Ramsons or wild garlic (*Allium ursinum*) likes the shade; this weed is unpopular because cows and goats that eat the plant produce tainted milk: second-hand garlic is never pleasant. In Yorkshire in my youth no one would dream of using wild garlic, but foragers look for it these days. In Europe, where people have traditionally valued weeds, it has always been gathered and used for flavouring. It is related to chives. The star-like flowers of ramsons have six white petals and are seen from April to June, when the plant is easier to find.

MAN-MADE WILDLIFE CORRIDORS

Important wildlife habitats are provided by railway lines, canals and motorways, all places where insects, birds and animals can live, breed and move about with little human interference. Translocation is vital for all creatures, which need to find new sources of food and somewhere to live once they have left the nest. Corridors like this are used to find a mate, and as the young mature, they will use them to move away from the parental nest to find a niche of their own.

Most people have seen birds of prey hovering over motorways; they find shelter in the extensive roadside verges and take advantage of road kill for food. Insects live on the wild flowers.

Canals harbour wildfowl, especially ducks, and many wetland weeds grow on their banks.

WETLAND HABITAT

There are many weeds that love boggy places, so it's good sometimes to leave a wet patch undrained, for the sake of the plants and also the wildlife. Damp, grassy areas may harbour water forget-me-not (*Myosotis scorpioides*), creeping jenny (*Lysimachia nummularia*), lady's smock, cuckoo flower or milkmaids (*Cardamine pratensis*) and as already mentioned, ragged robin. Cuckoo flower appears at the time of the first cuckoo, in April or May.

Canal banks are wildlife corridors.

Pond for wildlife.

Water Weeds

Ponds and streams add a great deal of interest to the countryside and have their own weed populations. Ponds without weeds are lifeless – although having said that, there are one or two exotic species of water weed that are undesirable because they tend to choke out the native vegetation and change the habitat. Some, such as Australian swamp stonecrop, used to be sold by nurseries but it is now illegal to supply them. One of the Lime Tree ponds is currently infested with this weed, and the advice is to fill in the pond and start again.

Aquatic weeds are often spread by waterfowl, so new ponds will soon acquire their own flora, for good or ill.

Duckweed (*Lemna* species), mentioned earlier, is a tiny perennial plant that floats, its rounded fronds attached to a hanging root. In some countries duckweed is harvested for animal food. This is the smallest flowering plant, although it doesn't flower often and tends to reproduce by means of buds on the edges of fronds. In winter, duckweed survives by producing buds that sink to the bottom of the pond.

Some plants grow entirely submerged in water. They are oxgenators, such as water milfoil (*Myriophyllum*) and water starwort (*Callitriche*), and provide oxygen and food for pond life. Some plants have roots in the water but their heads are above the water surface, and they give shelter and shade to amphibians.

Water mint (*Mentha aquatica*) is a strong-smelling perennial, and is another good nectar source for insects, even though the pink-mauve flowers are quite small. It can be used just like garden mint.

Water plantain is the name for a group of tall, broad-leaved perennial plants (*Alisma*). The

Pond infested with swamp stonecrop.

Duckweed.

leaves of some float, while others are submerged. The flowers are pale lilac in colour, and they shelter aquatic insects such as the many species of caddis fly.

Bur reeds (*Sparganium*) are found in the shallow water at the edge of ponds and streams. These perennial flowering plants are important members of the aquatic plant community, providing cover for waterfowl and their chicks, and food for several species. The flowers are spherical and whitish; the stems may be branched or single. Bur reed likes slow-moving water as it is liable to be uprooted by a fast-flowing stream.

Soft rush (*Juncus effusus*) is a tall, thin rush that provides food and nesting places for wildfowl and wading birds. It's common in boggy ground with plenty of humus. Rush lights and wicks for candles were once made from the inner pith of the stems, soaked in fat.

In the deeper shallows can be found reed mace (*Typha latifolia*), sometimes called bulrush. The brown seed heads are like sausages. Dragonflies lay eggs on this plant. The stems are used to weave baskets.

Yellow flag iris (*Iris pseudacorus*) is another plant of damp places, lighting up the margins of ponds with bright yellow flowers on a tall stem. The flowers are pollinated by long-tongued insects such as bumblebees as they reach for the nectar.

Marsh thistle (*Cirsium palustre*) is a tall thistle, sometimes growing up to 2 metres (7 feet) tall. It has purple flowers that are favoured by bees, and long, narrow, spiny leaves.

Water mint.

Yellow flag iris.

Willows round a replica of an Iron Age house at Lime Tree.

Willow weaving.

Willow (*Salyx* species)

Willow thrives in damp places; it is a plant with many uses. The leaves and bark were traditionally used in medicine, and its anti-inflammatory properties were eventually developed and used in the product aspirin. Willow grows fast, making it useful as fuel for energy production in biofuel systems. The long, pliant branches have been used for thousands of years to make baskets, fish traps, wattle fences and many other products, as they are less likely to split than the stems of other plants.

When a replica Iron Age house was built at Lime Tree, a willow fence was planted round it. This has grown and the stems are now ready for harvesting to make baskets.

Waste water is treated by filtering it through willows, and this helps the environment to cope with waste. Stream banks are stabilized with willow. (In Australia, however, willow is now being removed from the banks of creeks because it has become an invasive weed, changing the ecology of river systems.)

Pollen and nectar are produced when willow flowers, and the early pollen is welcome in spring when food for insects is scarce. People have been known to cook willow catkins and eat them in a hungry spring.

Bracken.

Moorland habitat.

UPLAND HABITAT

Plants and Wildlife

In hilly areas, bracken (*Pteridium*) is a persistent weed that can take over farmland unless it is kept in check, which is easier said than done. Bracken and heather (*Calluna vulgaris*) cover the moorland above our farm, in patches alternating with short moorland grasses grazed by sheep, and tiny flowers such as tormentil (*Potentilla erecta*). In late summer when the heather is in flower, beekeepers take hives up to the moor to harvest heather honey.

Bracken is one of the world's most widely distributed plants, providing cover for ground-nesting birds such as curlew, and food for many moths and butterflies. It also offers shelter to game birds such as pheasant and grouse.

Red grouse is a native upland bird, found

Broom and gorse.

in Scotland, Wales and the north of England; grouse live on the flowers, seeds and shoots of heather, and also eat bilberries and some insects. On moors where game is managed to produce an income, areas of heather are burned to encourage fresh shoots to feed the grouse; this practice also provides a supplementary food for sheep, and is an example of traditional weed management.

Bilberry (*Vaccinium myrtillus*) is so small and low growing it's easy to miss, but it is worth looking for on a sunny afternoon for its delicious tiny berries, one of the treats of late summer. Bilberries also feed other moorland birds and insects.

The common lizard often makes its home on moorland; you may see it basking in the sun on a stone, soaking up energy to allow it to hunt for food. Lizards live on invertebrates such as spiders, worms and snails; in turn they are eaten by birds of prey. They may hibernate in groups. Bracken and heather provide cover for lizards, and shelter the small creatures they depend on for food.

Gorse (*Ulex europaeus*) is a prickly shrub that covers the hillsides with a wash of yellow flowers, sometimes even in winter. In the past it was put to several uses. Cattle will avoid gorse in pastures, so to make it a palatable feed, farmers used to cut it and grind the shoots with stones or through a mill. Gorse burns well and was used for domestic fires and bakery ovens.

Gorse is important to several species of bird

in spite of its thorns, for nesting sites and protection. The linnet, stonechat and yellowhammer nest in gorse, and in particular it supports the Dartford warbler, a bird of southern Britain. Severe winters lowered the population levels of this little bird, and at one time it was on the endangered list; however, its numbers are now recovering.

The flowers of gorse provide nectar for many insects, and its long flowering habit makes it an important nectar source when other flowers are scarce.

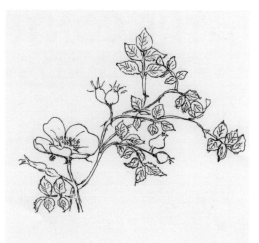

Wild rose.

6 THE CONTROL OF WEEDS

In spite of their benefits, weeds have to be managed. A piece of land left to itself will revert to the wild very quickly. Tall weeds grow up and die down, then shrubs move in, such as blackberry and wild rose; in upland areas the invaders may be bracken and gorse. They will give cover to tree seedlings, quite often hardy trees such as sycamore, which flies in with wings on its seeds.

In this section domestic animals are included as weed controllers because they can be very effective – *see* below. Feeding weeds to animals not only gets rid of the weeds, it provides food for the livestock and goes towards producing manure, milk, wool or meat.

The challenge is to find sustainable ways of getting rid of weeds. It's easy to spray, and as a last resort this may be needed, but chemical control is expensive and has its dangers. Herbicides are not supposed to harm people, but I know at least one farmer who suffered from headaches and depression after using sprays. No doubt the worms, beneficial fungi and all the other denizens of the soil also wake up with a headache after being drenched with spray, if they wake up at all.

There is a movement away from herbicides and towards more organic methods of controlling unwanted plants. More people are counting the

Hand hoeing on an organic farm.

cost of sprays in terms of human health, the effect on the environment, and the expense. Sometimes a chemical spray can inhibit the growth of the next crop planted in that soil.

HAND WEEDING

If you have a large area to weed, it could be safer and even cheaper to pay someone to pull them out. Hand weeding can be tedious, but it's effective for garden weeds. Certainly it is daunting when you're faced with a whole field of weeds, but pulling out weeds between rows of vegetables is the best form of control, and if you can leave them on the surface as a mulch, so much the better. Admittedly weeds left in an onion bed may mean a 'search and rescue' operation later on to find the onions, especially after a rainy period.

Field weeds can be taken out fairly easily by hand when the weeds are few and scattered. Thistles can be dug out before they set seed. In the days before universal chemical use, hand weeding was done on a field scale. Arable crops such as turnips were hoed by a team of workers moving slowly down the long rows, sometimes competing amongst themselves to see who could get to the end of the row first. Young Farmers Clubs ran hoeing competitions. More labour was available on mixed farms in those days, and wages were lower – and therefore more affordable for the farmer – than is the case today.

Hoeing is still a good option on small organic farms, where vegetable crops are often grown to sell at farmers' markets. At the same time as the weeds are killed, the plants can be 'singled' so that they grow at the right spacing.

Hold a Weed Party

Once we had a ragwort party: this was a social occasion with a barbecue, but before our friends were allowed to eat we gave them gloves and led the way to a delightful little valley. The slopes were covered with yellow ragwort flowers, but once we all set to work these were very soon removed, while everybody enjoyed the fresh air and exercise. It's a great way to get rid of weeds – although the penetrating ragwort smell seemed to linger with us after the job was over.

OTHER WAYS OF MANAGING WEEDS

Compete with Plants

One way to control weeds is to crowd them out with the plants you want to grow. Get in first with big leaves such as those of courgettes and marrows. Plant dwarf beans more closely than usual. Underneath orchard trees use nasturtiums – although these can be aggressive climbers at times, sometimes swamping smaller trees, which have to be rescued from their clutches. Fortunately nasturtiums have weak stems and are easy to pull away from their victims.

Broad beans grow through the cooler weather and they tend to sprawl when fully grown, so they cover the ground well and prepare it for a summer crop.

Rhubarb is a useful plant, with huge leaves that keep out weeds. It's a perennial and doesn't mind shade, so rhubarb can fill up a weedy corner and produce bright red stems for making chutney or rhubarb crumble. (Rhubarb leaves are poisonous, so don't give them to animals.)

Patches of marigold and borage are good on the edges of beds, where orthodox gardeners use a spray to keep down weeds.

Slashing or Mowing

Slashed weeds are used as a mulch on many organic farms and gardens. The grass and weeds between rows of berries or vines is cut and left to form a mulch to keep down further weed growth, conserve moisture and add nutrients to the soil. For some producers this means that they can manage without irrigation, which involves the use of further resources and just adds to the cost of production. Some organic farmers use little or no fertilizer, relying on weed nutrients to feed the soil.

Slashed weeds as mulch.

Nowadays there are tractor-towed 'mulchers' that cut the weeds higher than a grass mower would, allowing the grass to recover quickly. Once they have dried, the cut weeds are more likely to be eaten by livestock.

Plant Late

You might think it would be better to plant crops early, to get a head start, but in fact it's a good idea to plant later in the planting season rather than earlier, so the vegetables compete by growing strongly. For example, early beans may seem a good idea, but beans don't like a cold spring, and won't really take off until the ground warms up to at least 20°C. Neither will tomatoes, courgettes and many other vegetables, and while they struggle, the hardy weeds sneak in.

Green Manure Cover Crop

A common green manure seeds mixture consists of oats, vetch and barley, sown thickly on the ground and often netted until the seeds germinate to keep off the voracious birds. Leave it for a few weeks, and when you come back you'll have a green cover crop but no weeds. Dig it in and it will soon disappear. This is a popular mix for a green manure crop. Vetch is a legume, so it has nitrogen-fixing bacteria on its roots, adding nitrogen to the soil (as mentioned elsewhere). Barley makes phosphorus more available to the next crop, and oats are said to exude a chemical that suppresses weed growth.

A cheaper source of seeds for green manure is bird seed. I put in a patch of sunflower seeds in spring, to be slashed or dug in later. Green manure can be slashed and left on the surface as a mulch until you want to use the ground, when it can be dug in or moved to one side for planting a crop. Mulch, whether a green manure crop or weeds, will discourage weeds.

Solarization

The sun's heat can be used to kill weeds. If you block the light with a sheet of plastic, the heat will build up and cook the weeds. Use black plastic, bury the edges in the soil, and wait for at least a month. This works for annual weeds, though sometimes the deeper-rooted perennials put their heads up again when the cover is removed.

Sawdust

A thick layer of sawdust will kill weeds when it's fresh. Sawdust works well round shrubs, and I've used it with ferns. It eventually breaks down and adds to soil humus, though it steals nitrogen in the process. It can be used between rows of vegetables, but in this case needs to be watered frequently with 'weed tea', made by steeping weeds in water. I don't use sawdust very much in the vegetable garden, but it's useful round ornamental shrubs.

Boiling Water

Boiling water is lethal to plants. It's the best way to get rid of moss and weeds growing between paving stones or bricks, because once it cools

An abandoned garden soon reverts to the wild.

it is harmless to birds, children and pets. It is also effective against deep-rooted weeds such as docks. A kettle of water boiled on the wood stove is a cheap weedkiller, though don't use too big a container as boiling water is dangerous.

Cut Down on Sources of Weeds

Where are your weeds coming from? Many weeds can be introduced by animal manure. In a perfect world, composting manure before use would heat it to the point where all weed seeds were killed. But some get through, and unless you buy pelleted poultry manure in little bags, you will probably get some weeds in manure.

Cow manure sprouts grass weeds, unless it's from cattle that have been wintered in sheds – and even then it will harbour seeds from the animals' food.

Another source of weeds is hay, whether you buy it for a garden mulch or to feed stock. As a rule we make our own hay, but we suffered an outbreak of wild barley on our farm that was caused by bought-in hay. This weed makes a prickly mat that the cows avoid.

LIVESTOCK FOR WEED CONTROL

People who have room to keep domestic animals often use them for effective weed control. How-

A Gloucester Old Spot will eat weeds happily.

ever, there is quite a lot of work attached to livestock, and if you haven't much time, a lawnmower may be simpler than keeping sheep or even a pen of rabbits for weed control. One alternative is to borrow a neighbour's livestock at intervals to keep down weeds.

Managing Weeds with Pigs

If you feel you're losing the battle with big perennial weeds, outdoor pigs can come to the rescue. Years ago our family farmed in Wales where we had a hillside covered with bracken and gorse; this was very pretty when the gorse was flowering but it meant the land was not producing any grass for the cattle or sheep. The pigs soon changed all that. They joyfully rooted in the earth and removed both the gorse and the bracken, digging out the roots and finding other species of plant as well. Pigs have extremely strong noses and they love to dig – and they will eat almost anything. Of course, we also fed them on pig nuts (pig food designed to be fed outdoors, too big to be stolen by birds – except pheasants and rooks).

By the time the pigs and their moveable sleeping hut were moved on, we had a well tilled paddock, manured by the pigs and ready for grass seed. This is a drastic remedy because it removes all the green cover, but as a short-term solution it works very well. Wales has a high rainfall, but the slope helped to prevent the ground from becoming a mud bath.

Usually our sows were rotated round our paddocks, with rings in their noses to prevent digging. Like this, once they had tilled out the weeds, we were able to maintain a green cover, moving the pigs on frequently to graze on fresh grass without allowing them to dig over the whole farm! This is how outdoor pig farms are organized.

Pigs are intelligent animals and love the outdoor life. However, the modern hybrid types that are bred for intensive conditions may not be such good foragers as the old breeds we kept. If you are thinking of keeping pigs, try to find one of the rare breeds. Tamworth, Large Black, Saddleback and Gloucester Old Spot pigs are now endangered breeds, but if you can find them, they are tough and they will help you to manage rough patches of land. The Gloucester was known as the 'orchard pig', and was often used to keep down weeds in orchards and to eat the fallen apples.

The Rare Breeds Survival Trust (www.rbst. org.uk) will put you in touch with breeders of outdoor pigs.

Even a couple of fattening pigs in a cottage sty can convert some of your weeds into bacon. They are very fond of most weeds, and pigs confined to pens will really appreciate a handful of greenstuff every day, so hand weeding can also help to feed them.

Sheep

As mentioned before, sheep will eat young ragwort plants, and they will help with weed control, especially if they are confined to a small area. They are excellent lawn mowers. In some parts of the world, sheep are available to rent for this purpose!

Traditionally sheep are used to keep down weeds in orchards and sometimes in plantations of Christmas trees. The trees give shelter and shade to the animals. There is less impaction of the ground by machinery, and labour is saved as well as chemicals.

A farmer from Oregon, USA, told me that he practised 'two-tier farming', with sheep under cherry trees. He never needed to mow the grass, and the sheep manured the ground. There is now a revival of interest in using sheep to control weeds and pests in cider orchards in England, as farmers look for organic alternatives to sprays.

Sheep may like to nibble tree bark and the lower leaves of orchard trees, but if they are moved frequently and have plenty of food the effect will be minimized. One particular old breed, the Shropshire Down, is said to be suited to living in orchards. They keep down fungal infestations such as the dreaded apple scab by eating the fallen leaves. Various groups are studying the effect of sheep in orchards (*see* www.permaculture.co.uk/ articles).

Sheep weed control does not extend to nettles.

Goats

Goats do eat grass but they are browsers, which means they happily nibble shrubs and trees as high as they can reach by standing on their hind legs – which is not so good for orchards. They come into their own on blackberry-infested land and where there are woody shrubs to control. It was recently reported that parks in New York were using goats for weed control on inaccessible land. Goats themselves can be hard to control: they like to wander, and if given the chance will eat your garden as well as the weeds. They are hard to fence in. But few animals will nibble thistle heads as goats do.

A farmer who recruited some Boer goats to clear weeds on a farm I visited recently found that they didn't get on with the job – they just waited at the gate for him to feed them. But they were fat and I suspect he fed them so well that they didn't need the weeds.

By repeatedly nibbling away at the leaves, goats can kill blackberries. I've heard people say that the poor things must be starving to eat rough bushes, but in fact goats need roughage for their digestion to work properly, and more roughage than other ruminants. They need woody shrubs, rough vegetation, and plants that other livestock avoid. Of course if they are producing milk or being reared for their meat, they will need other food as well.

Goats trying thistle heads.

Cattle

Cattle are selective, and if they have a choice they prefer green, succulent leaves. Their soft mouths can't cope with prickles, and they don't like acid plants such as docks.

The best way to control weeds in cattle pastures is to ensure that the grass grows vigorously enough to crowd the weeds out. This will usually entail spreading fertilizer such as pig or poultry manure, and not allowing the cattle to graze the grass right down to the roots before moving them on. But without adequate rainfall, the hardy weeds will beat the grass species. Weeds on farms often result after a drought, although in gardens they may be more prevalent in wet seasons.

It's interesting that, in the same way as pigs and sheep, the old breeds of cattle cope best with weeds. The Dexter is an ancient small breed that originates from Ireland, and which has evolved over the centuries to live and thrive on poor land. They were fashionable in England in the nineteenth century, adorning the parks of stately homes. They are a minority breed but they have a devoted following all over the world, their small size making them popular with people on a small acreage, for both meat and milk. Those who keep them say they are very good weed suppressers, and will eat weeds with relish.

Poultry

Free-range hens will improve grass paddocks and eat a surprising amount of green food, including weeds. They will remove weed seeds, and even eat the bulbs of oxalis if they get the chance. Put into a small area of weed-infested land, chickens can clear it down to bare earth, as will pigs but on a smaller scale.

Dexter cattle.

If you can't let them range free, then a moveable ark will be the answer.

Once again, the old breeds will probably be better foragers than the chickens bred for an indoor life, but it is surprising how battery hens, once liberated, quickly learn the traditional chicken skills they've never enjoyed before.

Hens like sow thistle, chickweed and fat hen, especially when it carries seeds.

Ducks are weed eaters so they need access to water, and of course they like the duckweeds (for example *Lemna minor*). These are common weeds in ponds and watercourses, with the potential to provide food for other livestock. Duck-weeds are simple plants, floating on the surface of the water or just below it, and their protein content is one of the highest in the plant world, higher than that of soybeans. Duckweeds can remove water pollution, provide shelter for small aquatic creatures and reduce water evaporation.

These plants are eaten by humans in some parts of the world, and there is a worldwide interest in research to find ways of using them for food production, because they grow so fast. If your pond grows duckweed remember it's not a weed at all, it's a sign of a healthy pond. Too much can be a nuisance, covering the water surface, but ducks will control it.

Free-range hens will eat some weeds.

Geese need to be outdoors, grazing on green food, more than other species of poultry. Ours usually lived in an orchard, which they kept weed free. They like to live under trees, protected from hot sun. They love windfall apples, and get more of their nutrition from green food than hens. If they have a large enough area, they won't need much extra food during the growing season. When the growth dies down, you then need to give them extra food.

Turkeys are rather more demanding than other poultry and need a high protein diet, but they like brassica weeds, particularly if you are kind enough to hang them up so they can reach them easily.

Sow thistle.

7 WEEDS FOR HEALTH

Many of our so-called weeds have a long history as medicinal herbs. The lowest level of excavation in Shanidar cave in northern Iraq was found to hold the bones of a man buried 60,000 years ago. It is thought that his grave had been strewn with flowers. Pollen found on the site enabled the identification of eight species of plants that all still grow in the area, seven of which are still used for medicine by the local people. They include mallow and yarrow, familiar to us as weeds, and the shrub Ephedra, used in modern medicine (*see* Barbara Griggs' *Green Pharmacy*, Vermont USA 1997).

For thousands of years, herbs have been used from day to day, often by women. By the end of the nineteenth century herbalists were being attacked by the medical establishment, but in many districts, such as the industrial north of England, they were the only source of medical help available. My great-grandfather made herbal preparations for neighbours in Yorkshire; the only comment that has come down the years is that his pills were rather too big to swallow!

Chemical companies developed artificial drugs and isolated the active principles of plants so they had no need to gather plant material. Lowly weeds fell by the wayside except as 'cottage remedies'. Then there was a gradual movement back to an appreciation of the uses of plants. One book helped to turn the tide: *A Modern Herbal*, first published in 1931. It was written by Maud Grieve and edited by her colleague Hilda Leyel, and is now available to consult online. This monumental work contains what was known at the time about the value of plants, also some of the history of their use, and a selection of pronouncements by the old herbalists such as Culpeper.

Since then a gradual trickle of books about herbs has appeared, gradually turning into a flood. Herbs are in fashion again, even though cottage remedies may still be frowned upon by the orthodox. I am not suggesting that a decoction of weeds can replace professional advice, whether conventional or alternative. But for mild ills such as bites, scratches or indigestion, or for twinges of arthritis, it's good to know that a remedy might be growing in your garden.

The list of minerals and vitamins contained in weed species is impressive. It's worth noting that some scientists believe there has been a drop in omega-3 fatty acids in our food plants since they have been bred for a long shelf life. We usually associate omega 3 with fish oil, but it's all derived from plants and passed on by the fish. Weeds such as purslane contain a high amount of this fatty acid.

HERBAL PREPARATIONS

The mortar and pestle were standard equipment for a country kitchen, and were also the

Mortar and pestle traditionally used for pounding herbs.

apothecary's tools. The mortar is a bowl made of stone or hardwood, and the pestle is a blunt-ended, heavy object used to grind or crush herbs, seeds or other substances in the bowl.

This section summarizes the different ways in which herbs are most commonly prepared and used as medicine. Eating them, especially raw in salads, is the simplest, but there are many country cures embodied in the weeds growing around us that can be used in traditional ways.

Drying: Dried Herbs

Most leaves and flowers can be used fresh or dried. Drying concentrates the active principles, and also means that you can store the material for use when needed, or when the plant is not available, for instance in the winter months.

For drying, plants should be picked when fresh and young and after the morning dew has dried. They can be laid out on newspaper in a warm, dry room, or hung in bunches in an airy place. Roots can be cleaned and dried in an oven with the door partly open to let out the moisture; however, this isn't a good idea for aromatic herbs. Berries can also be dried for winter use.

Dried plant material should never be stored in plastic: it is best kept out of the light, and stored in a paper bag or a glass jar with a lid. If you haven't used it by the time the next growing season comes round, scatter the dried leaves in the garden, or add them to compost.

Infusion: Herb Tea

The easiest way to take weeds for health is probably as a cup of weed tea. A cup of herb tea is made by scalding fresh or dried leaves in boiling water, then letting it stand for a few minutes: this is an infusion. Dried leaves are useful, as they can be

Dried hawthorn berries used to make hawthorn tea.

Dried mint.

stored easily and will give you a stronger brew. A couple of teaspoons of the herb to a cup of water is a common recommendation. A mixture of herbs, or herbs and dried fruit, can be made to suit your own taste.

Herbalists say that making the brew in a teapot with the lid on will ensure that essential oils are not lost by evaporation. Herb teas can be drunk hot or cold, and are usually taken without milk. Honey is the best sweetener. They can be mixed with fruit juices as a healthy way to drink more water. You can also make an infused oil.

Decoction

A decoction is made by boiling the herb in water, to release more of its constituents and make it more effective; how long it is boiled for depends on what it is made of. This method is useful for extracting the goodness from seeds, bark, roots or tough leaves – tough plants may need to be boiled for hours.

Maceration

Maceration is a cold infusion, used when the plant contains a lot of volatile oils or mucilage, such as mallow. The dried herb is steeped in cold water overnight, then strained and heated before drinking.

Making a Tincture

To make a tincture, plant material is soaked in oil, vinegar or, say, 80 proof alcohol (the strength depending on what you want to extract) such as vodka, to extract the relevant constituents. Our herbalist says: 'One part plant to five parts liquid is usual with dried material to reflect the fresh plant, as plants are usually composed of 80 per cent water.'

A glass jar is filled with the chopped herb, fresh or dried, then topped up with the liquid and left to stand at room temperature, but out of the sun, for at least six weeks. The liquid can then be decanted into a dark glass jar or bottle. You now have a concentrated extract of the herb in a convenient form for storage. Tinctures are used in small amounts, such as a spoonful of medicinal vinegar.

Compress

A compress can be applied to the skin to help healing; it is made by soaking a clean cotton or linen cloth with the appropriate herb tea. It is usually applied hot for greatest effect, and is held in place with another cloth.

Poultice

A poultice consists of a paste of bruised fresh leaves, or dried herbs mixed to a paste with hot water. The poultice can be put straight on to the skin, or sandwiched between two layers of thin material such as gauze. A drop or two of oil makes it easier to remove afterwards.

Ointments

To make an ointment, first infuse an oil such as olive oil with the chopped plant material to be used. Cover the material in a jar with hot or cold oil, seal the jar, and leave for about two weeks until the oil is coloured. Strain and bottle. Next, heat beeswax gently in the infused oil until the two merge; the mixture will become more solid as it cools. Beeswax can be difficult to handle if it solidifies in the wrong place, as, for example, candlewax on your dining table.

Creams and Lotions

These preparations consist of the herb of choice and oil- and water-based ingredients, technically an emulsion. Again, beeswax can be used as an emulsifier; alternatively a strong tea can be beaten up with a commercial handcream to make a soothing cream. Once again, be very sure that you identify correctly the plant you intend to use, and take medical advice when you need it.

Freezing

Herbalist John Earnshaw suggests freezing as a good way to preserve plant material, for example aloe vera. It can be frozen in ice cubes; applying the remedy cold will also help to reduce inflammation.

A SELECTION OF PLANT REMEDIES

Plantain for First Aid

Plantain is astringent and anti-inflammatory, which makes it useful in several ways for first aid in the field. Traditionally, plantain leaves were used to stop bleeding from cuts by the men who mowed grass with scythes, because the juice has coagulating properties. Fresh plantain leaves can be chewed and then rubbed on the skin to soothe bites or stings, including nettle stings, or they can be used to make a soothing cream. Chewing releases the active principle.

As a valuable medical herb, plantain is used to make a tea for indigestion, for example mixed with mint, another treatment for indigestion. It is anti-microbial, and internally, plantain has been used to treat diarrhoea, giardia and other infections. It used to be an old remedy for water retention, as in swollen ankles, as a tea, also made with the addition of dandelion and nettle leaves.

Marigold petals to be pounded for ointment.

Yarrow or Milfoil

Yarrow or milfoil is a common weed of grassland. It is a traditional herbal treatment for several ills, and is mentioned above as one of the plants found at a Neanderthal burial site. Yarrow's old names include woundwort, indicating that country folk found its astringency useful to stop bleeding. The leaves and flowers are used and can be dried in summer for later use. It is best picked when flowering, when it is easy to identify.

Yarrow tea is a good remedy for colds and flu, and also for rheumatism. It contains salicylic acid (aspirin), which is a painkiller and reduces a high temperature. The taste is bitter so it's more palatable when sweetened with honey, but the astringency of the tea is helpful in cases of indigestion or diarrhoea. Yarrow makes you sweat and in doing so reduces body temperature. John Earnshaw recommends a mix including yarrow and elderflower for sweating out a virus.

Goosefoot or Fat Hen

Goosefoot has anti-inflammatory properties. A poultice made from the leaves can be applied to superficial burns and insect bites and stings. The juice of the stem soothes sunburn.

Narrow-leaved plantain.

Rocket Salad

The medicinal virtues of rocket are similar to those of broccoli, which is now regarded as a wonder food. Both plants contain the molecule sulforaphane, which has anti-bacterial and anti-cancerous properties, and also blocks the enzymes that cause joint destruction, so it helps to slow down or prevent some forms of osteoarthritis. Since much of this substance is destroyed by cooking, raw rocket must be one of the best sources.

Comfrey

Comfrey cream or ointment is a fast healer because it contains allantoin, which encourages cell regrowth and wound healing. It is soothing and anti-irritant. Allantoin is used commercially in cosmetics. I have used comfrey over many years and have been surprised at the speed with which it helps healing. I use comfrey leaves, but many herbalists use the root, dried and powdered.

This plant is not now recommended for internal use, although vegans used to take it because it's about the only plant source of vitamin B12. PA, the toxic alkaloid mentioned in a previous section, was isolated from comfrey and was then found to poison laboratory rats, which cast a dark shadow on the plant's reputation.

Many common vegetables contain potential toxins, but are safe unless you eat them to excess. Comfrey may be in the same class, but the leaf is rough and hairy and the taste is rather oily. It is banned for internal use in the UK, and should be particularly avoided if you are pregnant.

Nasturtium flowers in vinegar.

Nasturtiums

Nasturtium vinegar is made like any other herb vinegar: add some flowers and leaves to a jar of wine vinegar with a clove or two of garlic, and wait for about a month. Herbalists recommend a teaspoon twice a day to relieve catarrh.

If you want the benefits immediately, try adding nasturtiums to a salad.

Calendula Marigold

Calendula marigold is counted as a weed because although marigold is a garden flower, it spreads easily and can appear unexpectedly both in and outside the garden.

You can buy or make several preparations of this herb: lotions, ointments, salves and creams. Calendula is antiseptic and soothing, and also reduces swellings and bruises. It takes away the pain of stings and bites, and cures infected sites. The flowers have some anti-bacterial effect and also reduce inflammation. Calendula is anti-fungal as a tincture with 90 per cent proof alcohol.

Collect the flowers in the morning after the dew has dried, and separate the petals between sheets of paper to dry in a warm and shady spot. Once I was bitten by several insects and so I made a quick remedy, just pounding up marigold petals with a basic moisturizer to make a lemon-coloured ointment. It worked so well that I soon forgot about the bites.

For a longer-keeping salve, fill a small jar with marigold petals and cover them with good quality olive oil. Seal the jar and leave it in a warm place for a few weeks until the oil takes on the marigold colour. Strain out the petals and bottle. To make an ointment, add beeswax to the oil and warm over a low heat to melt the wax. Then pour the mixture into jars before it sets.

Marigold petals in oil.

Blackberry

Blackberry leaves contain a high level of tannin, making them a useful treatment for diarrhoea and dysentery; raspberry leaves have similar properties. A good herb tea can be made by infusing equal quantities of blackberry, raspberry and mint leaves together.

Blackberry vinegar used to be prescribed for a feverish cold. To make it, fill a bowl with clean blackberries and pour in malt vinegar until the berries are covered. After about three days, strain the mixture through a sieve. Measure the liquid and add a kilogram of sugar per litre. Mix until the sugar is dissolved and boil for about five minutes. Cool and bottle. Mix a teaspoonful in water for a pleasant drink.

Hawthorn

A tea can be made from the leaves or berries of hawthorn, and tastes quite pleasant. Hawthorn berries are common in early autumn, but if there are none in your area the dried product can be bought from herbal suppliers.

Hawthorn is highly valued as a heart tonic; it is said to regulate the heart function and support the cardiovascular and circulatory systems, normalizing high or low blood pressure. The herbalists say that it opens coronary arteries. It is supposed to help dissolve calcium and cholesterol deposits, which is good news for older bodies; it is also a mild sedative.

Taken as a preventative medicine hawthorn tea is safe, but people with heart problems need to take advice and check whether the tea is compatible with their medication. Pregnant women should avoid it.

Hawthorn cordial is made from the flowers, and as fresh ones are best, it's a seasonal treat. Pick fresh flowers, remove any insect life, and cut off the stems. For five cups of flowers, dissolve two cups of sugar in two cups of water, and boil for three minutes. Add the flowers, return to the boil, and then take off the heat. Add the juice of two lemons, cool and bottle. Diluted with water or soda water, this is a delicious medicine.

Chickweed

Even more than its food value, chickweed is valued as an important herbal medicine. This plant doesn't dry well, so it is used fresh. It is cooling and soothing, both internally and externally. I've seen this at first hand, having used a chickweed poultice to help heal wounds on a pig that had been fighting above its weight and needed help. The pig ate some of the chickweed, but I managed to poultice the wound, washing handfuls of the weed and applying it to the damaged area. The animal quickly recovered.

Chickweed ointment is a very good anti-itch cream for dermatitis or eczema.

Chickweed tea is recommended for many complaints, including peptic ulcers. Pour a cup of boiling water on to two to three teaspoons of fresh chickweed and let it stand for about ten minutes, then strain. Because it grows close to the ground, it's best to take special care with washing the plant before use. Once again, be very sure that you identify the plant correctly, and take medical advice when you need it.

Dandelion

Dandelion leaves or roots are used to make a tea for treating liver complaints. The roots are roasted to make a coffee substitute, and many herbalists sell dandelion coffee. Its main use is as a detoxifying treatment for the liver. Dandelion leaf is, of course, a diuretic, helping the body to get rid of excess water – hence the old English name 'pissabed', taken from French *pissenlit*. It is a good source of potassium.

Dandelion coffee is good for gall bladder problems. To make it, collect a bucketful of dandelion roots and wash them several times. Slice them into chips and dry in a dehydrator, or in an oven with the door slightly open to allow the moisture to escape. Roast in the oven until they are brown and completely dry, say thirty minutes at 200°C. Grind and then roast again for about five minutes at 180°C. Store in an airtight container.

Dandelion.

To serve, pour boiling water over several spoonfuls of grounds and leave for half an hour to infuse. You can add a cinnamon stick for a spicy flavour. Some people take their dandelion coffee with honey, others with cream.

ADDITIONAL HEALTHY GREENS, SALADS AND TONICS

(*See* Chapter 9 for more.)

We have seen that many weeds are used in salads and as green vegetables. They are especially useful at times when fresh food is scarce, because weeds will often keep on growing where cultivated plants fail. A regular intake of vitamin C is essential for health, and this is only one of the valuable contributions of greens to the diet. In times of war or floods, weeds have helped to keep people healthy when supplies of fresh food have been cut off. Rose hips were gathered from hedgerows in World War II (often by children paid to do the job) and made into a syrup to distribute to families.

Shepherd's Purse (*Capsella bursa-pastoris*)

Shepherd's purse is found all over the world except in the tropics, and was a famous cure for dysentery in the seventeenth century. It's another colonizer, appearing as a small plant in very poor ground, whilst in good soil it will grow to nearly half a metre. The young leaves are quite palatable;

the seeds are peppery. Mrs Grieve says that 'the leaves used to be sold as greens in Philadelphia in the spring.' This is another case of a plant that has gone down in the world.

The leaves are toothed and lie flat on the ground, rather like some other weeds, but the heart-shaped seedpods are unmistakable. Shepherds and other country folk carried leather pouches of this shape, made from the scrotum of a ram, which is where the name came from.

A tea made from the dried leaves of shepherd's purse is used to stop bleeding of all kinds, both internal and external. The plant is astringent and contains vitamin K, which the body needs to make proteins required for blood clotting. Cotton wool soaked in the tea can be used to stop a nosebleed. The weed was used in World War I to stop bleeding.

There is a long list of other uses of this plant, as a tonic, diuretic and a regulator of blood pressure. This is one of the herbs best avoided during pregnancy.

Cleavers (*Galium aperine*)

Cleavers climbs and clings by means of small hairs on its leaves and stems. If you brush past the plant it sticks to your clothes, which is its way of dispersing the seeds.

We were told that you can make coffee from the seeds of this plant, but although they do contain caffeine, they are so small that we soon gave up the attempt. It's also called goosegrass because geese are supposed to like the seeds. You can strain milk through a mat of cleavers, and you can stuff a mattress with it, but these old uses are hardly relevant now. However, this is a tonic plant, and it is recommended to take it as a tea, to detoxify the body. It is used as a wash to treat sunburn and skin irritations. It makes a useful green vegetable, too hairy for a salad but fine once cooked. Cleavers tea helps swollen lymph glands and gets the lymphatic system moving.

Medicinal Uses of Nettles

It's thought that the Romans spread the use of nettles in their travels round the world, especially in cold countries, as flogging the skin with nettles (urtification) was a rather painful way to stimulate the circulation and alleviate rheumatic pain. The medicinal uses of the plant are varied; nettle tea is obtainable at health food shops and is recommended for several applications – for example it may help to prevent seasonal allergies. It is recommended for urinary tract disorders and contains a compound, beta-sitosterol, which is said to lower the absorption of fats by the blood.

It is simple to dry the clean young leaves to make your own nettle tea, the form in which it is most commonly used as a medicine.

Raw nettle juice mixed with honey is said to help relieve the symptoms of asthma and bronchitis. It contains lots of minerals and is used as a counter-irritant. Nettle is rich in silica. Herbalists use the roots to treat an enlarged prostate.

Burdock (*Arctium minor*)

Burdock is remembered in Britain as an ingredient of a drink, dandelion and burdock, made since the Middle Ages from the fermented roots of both weeds. However, the commercial drink is now often made with artificial flavourings and no trace of the weeds: check the label to find out.

Burdock has large leaves with a lighter underside, and purple flowers in its second year. The seeds are burrs, which stick to animals and clothing – and they gave inventor Georges Mistral the idea for Velcro fastening.

Burdock roots and leaves can be boiled to make a blood purifier and, it's said, an excellent cure for eczema, used internally and also as a wash for skin disorders. It's oily and makes skin feel smoother. It is antibiotic and a mild laxative.

Feverfew (*Tanacetum parthenium*)

Feverfew is a little plant in the daisy family that grows wild, as well as being found in herb gardens. It is short, with daisy-like flowers and bright green leaves. Herbalists make an extract with the

Feverfew.

THE WEED MEDICINE CUPBOARD

It is not always convenient to go out foraging for weeds, especially when you have a cough or a cold. A stock of prepared remedies can be useful for these times, and also in winter, when many of our weeds disappear. Here are a few suggestions:

- Yarrow: dried leaves to make a tea to treat colds and flu
- Elderberry cordial for winter chills and viruses
- Elderberry flowers for allergies
- Dried comfrey leaves for comfrey ointment
- Young nettle leaves dried for tea, which has many benefits, according to herbalists
- Roasted and dried dandelion root, for dandelion coffee detox, and gallstones
- Dandelion leaf
- Nasturtium vinegar for catarrh
- Wild mint tea for indigestion
- Meadowsweet, a herbal painkiller
- Feverfew for migraine

fresh plant to treat migraines, an old remedy that was verified in the 1980s. Feverfew contains a substance called parthenolide, which is thought by some to inhibit the release of the hormone serotonin, believed to trigger migraine. A bitter tea can be made from the leaves and flowers, but the simplest way to take it is to eat three or four fresh leaves every day.

This herb may only be effective if you take it over a long period, such as six months.

Consult the Herbals

There are many more medicinal applications of weeds, as you may discover if you consult the herbals. As time goes by, more medicines will no doubt be produced from weeds. As Emerson said, a weed is 'a plant whose virtues have not yet been discovered.' We could add '...or a plant forgotten, waiting to be rediscovered.'

Plantain.

8 WEEDS AS VEGETABLE DYES

In the past, dyes were obtained from both cultivated and wild plants, and many weeds are still used for dyeing, producing attractive colours when used with natural fibres.

Dyes have coloured fabrics and brightened peoples' lives for thousands of years, probably beginning in ancient China. One might imagine early communities wearing homespun cloth in subdued hues, but scraps of material that have been preserved show us that our ancestors loved colour. Colour gives fabric individuality, which is why home dyeing still persists among people who like to design their own clothes.

In the past colour could confer status: for example, purple was the choice for Roman emperors, partly because it was very expensive to make. Imperial purple was obtained from a type of shellfish. Until the nineteenth century dyes were always made from natural substances, usually plants, but some came from lichens and also small animals. Cochineal is made from a scale insect native to South America.

Basket of nettles for dyeing.

Dyeing was traditionally a skilled occupation, with secret recipes that were carefully guarded. In Ireland it seems to have been secret women's business, and men were not allowed near the dye vat.

Quite early in the history of civilization some plants were cultivated for dyeing purposes – for example woad (*Isatis tinctoria*), the leaves of which produce indigo blue. This is the most important dye plant in the world. Roman generals reported facing blue hordes of British natives, assumed to have been stained with woad, and generations of Boy Scouts have sung the Woad Song, about how we Brits frightened our enemies by dyeing our skins blue.

There is just one commercial producer of woad in Britain now, based in Norfolk (*see* www.thewoadcentre.co.uk). It is still grown commercially in the Languedoc area of France. In King County, Washington, USA, where dyer's woad was once grown commercially, it is now classified as a noxious weed. Although woad was tried on our Yorkshire farm at one time, appropriately planted near the Iron Age house, it died out – it probably didn't like the winter frosts. Woad is a plant in the brassica family, which means it likes an alkaline soil and plenty of nitrogen.

The leaves to be used for dyeing are cut with secateurs in August, before there is any chance of frost, which can bleach them of colour. The stalks contain no dye, so dyers just use the leaves. To extract the dye, the leaves are put into hot – but not boiling – water for about ten minutes at 80°C.

Weld (*Reseda luteola*), also called dyer's weed, is another dye plant grown in the south of England, and it can still be found as a weed, mainly in the south and east. It was once common on the Sussex Downs, and it may still be worthwhile to hunt for it there, although originally it came from Mediterranean countries. Weld yields a yellow dye, best made from the fresh leaves. The plant has thin, tall spikes of yellowish-white or green flowers; this plant is a mignonette and has a sweet scent, which is used in perfumes and pot-pourris. Apparently it can be over-dyed with woad to produce Robin Hood's Lincoln Green (*see* www.wildcolours.co.uk for more on weed dyes).

Madder (*Rubia tinctorum*) yields a red dye from its roots, the pigment alizarin. Traces of this ancient dye were found in Tutankhamen's tomb, and dyeing enthusiasts are still growing it today. It has been used for colouring horses' hooves and women's fingernails. Madder was once used as animal fodder, and it is possible to find specimens growing as weeds.

The dye industry changed forever when an eighteen-year-old chemist, William Henry Perkin (1838–1907), accidently discovered the first aniline dye. He was trying to synthesize quinine, the treatment for malaria, when he discovered 'mauveine'. Young Perkin applied for a patent, and his career was made. Synthetic dyes began to appear in the mid-nineteenth century, and have almost completely replaced plant dyes for commercial purposes because they give the same result every time.

However, plant dyes remained popular with country spinners and knitters; they were popular in the hippy 1960s, and they are now an accepted part of the self-sufficiency movement. Dyeing is not an exact science when you work with weeds, but it can be fun to experiment. Many weeds can be used to make dyes for fabrics, but the colour may vary with the plants used, the time of year, the type of water, the process and the mordant (a substance used to fix the colour), not to mention the fabric. Nettle and dandelion were two dyes that we used in the past, to give us green and red colours, respectively.

People can get very technical about dyeing, but there are simple country recipes used by our ancestors that are still relevant today. With blackberries, for instance, a young woman could change the colour of her dress to pink or purple at no expense. During World War I when supply lines were blocked, German army uniforms were made from nettle cloth, and nettle dye was used to colour them – a striking instance of the value of weeds.

Scottish tartans were traditionally dyed with local plants, often weeds. From an early date alum was used as a mordant to fix the colour, as was also probably stale urine and/or wood ash. Examples of weeds used include dock, which

Dandelion flower.

produced black; dulse, a seaweed that was also eaten, which made a brown dye; dandelion gave magenta; while bracken and heather yielded yellow, according to the Scottish Tartans Authority.

PREPARING TO DYE

There is much to learn about plant dyes, and dyeing makes a fascinating hobby. This section is just an indication of what is waiting for you in the dyer's world, if you think of trying this use of weeds. Only natural fibres will take plant dyes. Wool is easier to dye than cotton, as I found when I tried to dye a cotton shirt.

You could start with dyeing an old garment to give it a new lease of life. In the case of a group in our village, dyeing followed on from learning to spin. We learned to spin and weave wool during lessons we took from a professional weaver, who worked with an eighteenth-century hand loom in a very old tradition. Some of us had the luxury of a whole fleece, but others were foragers, taking bits of wool from hedges and fences in sheep pastures and on moorland. This often made for an interesting mix of wool.

Once we had spun a skein of wool, we had to work out how to dye it. The choice was between synthetic and natural dyes, and we found that natural plant dyes gave much more attractive results, although they were less predictable.

Wool can be dyed in the fleece, in the skein, or after weaving; if you dye it in the skein you can weave or knit several colours together. For spinning we found that unwashed wool with the lanolin still in it was easier to spin, so we dyed after spinning, first thoroughly washing or 'scouring' the wool to get rid of the grease.

To prepare the dye, the plants are mashed up

and soaked in water overnight, or longer if possible. Tough plants may need days to soak. Roughly equal amounts of plant material and wool are needed. A good way is to crush the plants and put them in a stainless-steel container, then pour boiling water over them and leave them for three days, stirring up the mixture each day. Then strain off the water into a dye bath.

Mordants

Most vegetable dyes will wash out again, but you want your fabric to be washable and not to fade in the sun so the dye is usually fixed with a mordant, which gives fabric a ground for the colour to stick to. Some plant materials, such as lichens, do not need a mordant: these are called substantive dyes. More common are dyes that do need a fixative, called adjective dyes. The same plant material may give different colours with different mordants.

Salt, vinegar and rusty nails to provide iron were favourite mordants with traditional home dyers, although the process tended to be rather hit and miss. Salt often makes the colour brighter. Rhubarb leaves can be boiled up to make a mordant.

Alum is probably the most reliable mordant, but is not available over the counter now in Britain as far as I know, although you can buy it over the internet. Its full name is aluminium potassium sulphate. Many dye recipes specify alum; some also suggest you add Glauber's salts (sodium sulphate), a chemical that occurs naturally and is also a by-product of some chemical processes. Using this chemical causes the dye to penetrate the fabric more evenly.

THE DYEING PROCESS

The dyeing process starts with 'scouring' – washing your fabric so that the dye will stick, using gentle soap and rainwater if possible. The next stage is mordanting. You can use salt, vinegar, copper sulphate or alum in the following quantities.

To 13.5 litres of soft water, add either:

1½ cups salt
Or 6 cups vinegar
Or 85g alum – the most effective
Or 85g copper sulphate

Also used are tin (stannous chloride) and chrome (potassium bichromate), which must be handled with care.

Dissolve the mordant in the water, which should be warm but not hot. Then put the wet wool into it, bring to the boil and immediately turn down to a simmer. Simmer for an hour, then fish out the wool and rinse in hot water (sudden temperature changes are bad for wool).

After the wool has drained, put it straight in the dye bath and simmer the wool in the dye for an hour. If there is not enough dye solution to cover the wool, add water to top it up.

Hat dyed with lichen.

Only natural fibres will take a plant dye, so if you twist in a synthetic fibre with your wool this will emerged undyed. Colours will vary a lot, so it may be hard to match one batch with another – but it may not matter. If it does, it might pay to dye all you need at one go, which could require a big cauldron or a bucket on top of the stove. One pound of wet wool will need about 3 gallons of dye.

It is also possible to combine mordanting and dyeing, and add the mordant to the dye bath.

Recently I dyed a white cotton shirt with nettles. The young, bright green nettles produced a brilliant green in the dye bath, but I was not able to get hold of alum, which is the recommended mordant. I used vinegar instead, and followed the process outlined above – but instead of the bright green I hoped for, the shirt emerged from the bath a pleasant creamy colour.

DYEING WITH LICHENS

There are many species of lichen, and some of them produce excellent dyes; they are plentiful in Scotland, and they, too, were used for tartan colours. Lichens contain acids that yield their colours without the need for a mordant: they are substantive dyes. We might think of lichens as weeds – they often need to be removed from gravestones – but they're not plants: they are an association of two different organisms depending on each other, a fungus and an alga, a tiny plant-like organism. The fungus provides shelter, and the alga, food.

Crotal, or crottle, is the name for several types of rock lichen used in Scotland and Ireland. One such is *Parmelia saxatilis*, a greenish-grey lichen often found on exposed rocks, which produces a range of reddish-brown colours. Children used

Lichen on a rock.

to be sent out to collect crottle after rain, when it was easier to prise it from the rocks.

According to one source, if you dip a small piece of your lichen in household bleach, it will change colour to that of the dye it will yield, possibly pink or purple.

In damp places lichen grows on stonework, on walls and on the sides of trees. It might be interesting to boil some up and then try it as a dye. For pinks or reds, the recipe is to soak the lichen for about three months in a 2:1 solution of ammonia and water. A simpler method is to boil it up like other weeds, in which case it may yield a yellow or brown dye. The Harris tweed colours are said to have been obtained with lichen, which also imparts the traditional smell.

An Example of Lichen Dyeing

Norman Bush teaches rural crafts such as rope making at country shows, and he loves practical self-sufficiency, which sometimes extends to him making his own clothes and shoes. When he acquired a sheep's fleece he decided to make a jacket and hat, and to dye them with lichen. The wool was spun and woven for the jacket, and he used a felting process to make the hat.

Lichen was chosen for the dye because it wouldn't need a mordant, and also because Norman wanted a russet colour for his garment. He collected crottle lichen and boiled it for about two hours in a cloth bag, then strained off the liquid and cooled it. He dyed the wool in the skein, after spinning but before weaving.

He put the wool into his dye bath and raised the temperature gradually, then simmered the wool in the dye for about an hour. It was allowed to cool before it was removed from the bath, then rinsed and dried. The resulting colour is like autumn leaves: Norman can fade away into the autumn woods. Plant dyes, naturally enough, are perfect for blending in with the countryside.

Norman dyed his coat with lichen.

WEEDS FOR DYEING

There are many weeds used for dyeing, so you should be able to select one or two wherever you live. The chemicals that produce colour are many and varied, but natural dyes will vary with the season and even the weather, so even with a chemistry degree it's not always possible to predict the result. Natural dyeing is more of an adventure than a predictable process.

Alizarin: A purple dye present in several plants, most noticeably in madder. It can now be produced synthetically. Some of the dye plants occur elsewhere in this book as they are valuable in other ways in addition to yielding colour. It has been suggested that woad and madder were probably cultivated for medicinal use.

Yarrow: Yields a yellow dye with alum and cream of tartar. Flavones (*flavus* is Latin for yellow) in some plants are natural antioxidants and may protect against cancer. They also yield yellow and green dyes, which are said to work better in water that is slightly alkaline. Quercetin and luteolin are flavonols found in yarrow. Luteolin in particular has a very long history as a dyestuff.

Blackberry: The berries or young shoots give a pink or purple dye with alum.

Bracken: Young shoots or old tops give yellow or green with alum.

Elder: The leaves, berries and bark will give yellow or grey with iron or alum.

Ivy: The berries give yellow or green with alum or iron.

Cleavers and the related **lady's bedstraw** (*Galium verum*)**:** Both produce a red dye with alum,

Cleavers gives a red dye with alum.

the colour being extracted from the roots in a warm bath. In the past lady's bedstraw was dried and used to stuff mattresses, another use for weeds! The plant contains a chemical, coumarin, which gives off the scent of new mown hay; it also has the advantage that it kills fleas. It would have made a fragrant medieval mattress. Madder, mentioned above, is one of the bedstraws.

Lichen: Various types, as mentioned above. One gives pink with washing soda as a mordant. Lichens were often used for dyeing in the past, but they don't give up their colour easily, and were fermented or boiled. The traditional method of fermentation was to leave the plant for weeks or months in urine. This is said to be a method used in Scotland to produce the colours needed for weaving tartans. Modern equivalents are ammonia and lime.

Nettle leaves: Make green or yellow with alum.

Ragwort: The flowers give a deep yellow dye with alum.

Gypsywort (*Lycopus europaeus*): A black dye. This is a perennial that looks a little like mint, with jagged leaves and small white flowers in groups where the leaves join the stem. It grows in wet areas by the side of ponds, mainly in the south. Gypsywort was supposed to be used by gypsies to darken their skin, hence the name, although the motive for this is obscure.

Rhubarb leaves: Yield a yellow dye. The oxalic acid in the leaves, which is in toxic amounts, helps to fix the dye.

Dandelion.

9 EATING WEEDS

If you can't beat 'em, eat 'em! This is a good motto for gardeners who battle with weeds. A great many of our weeds are edible, as we have seen already, and fit into favourite recipes in place of cultivated vegetables, especially greens. Now that foraging is so popular it's easy to find weed recipes, in books or online. There are precautions to take when using weeds in recipes, but it's really a matter of common sense. Make sure you have identified the plant correctly and that no contamination has occurred. There are some very good books and web sites with descriptions and photographs of both edible and poisonous plants. If in doubt, leave it out.

This section gives just a small selection from the thousands of wild weed recipes. Using weeds for food is part of our social history. A glimpse of past ages can be found in the recipes, from times when people were closer to the wild, when they went short of food in bad seasons, or when they cultivated plants that have since become weeds.

On many occasions weeds came to the rescue when famine threatened a community, such as silverweed (*Potentilla anserina*, or *Argentina anserina*). The fleshy roots of this weed can be cooked as a vegetable or ground up to make a meal to make bread or porridge. Silverweed was once cultivated for its starch content.

Rose hips provided vitamin C for children in World War II (*see* below).

SOUPS

Wild Herb Soup

A French tradition, wild herb soup is celebrated by Emilie Carles in her autobiography of that name (first published in French in 1977). She describes walking by the river near her home, Briançon in the Alps of south-eastern France, gathering plants for her soup. She lists rib grass (plaintain), wild sorrel, *drouille* (a mountain herb), nettle, salsify, dandelion, lamb's lettuce, sedge, yarrow,

---

WEED FORAGING GUIDELINES

- Pick young plants and use the growing tips; avoid them if they look dried up or 'past their use-by date'
- Before flowering is usually the best time for greens, but some flowers can be eaten
- Older plants are more likely to harbour insects
- Stems and roots are often too fibrous and tough to eat, but not always
- Watch out for pollution in all its forms: herbicides, insects, traffic fumes, animal manure, bird droppings, dirty water and pets, especially roaming dogs that visit your weeds
- Unless you are ridding your patch of weeds, take only a proportion of plants and leave some to propagate for the future

Rose hips.

tetragonia (we call it New Zealand spinach), a sage leaf, a sprig of chive. Then she adds a touch of garlic, a few potatoes or a handful of rice. Like many wild recipes, this one will vary with the seasons and with what's in the larder.

Nettle Soup

Nettles can be added to almost any vegetable soup, contributing their own distinctive flavour. Gather about two cups of young nettle tops, wash them and cut off the tough stalks. Chop up a couple of leeks, an onion and two sticks of celery, and cook them in butter gently until they soften. Add a litre of vegetable or chicken stock and a handful of white rice. Simmer for about ten minutes, then stir in the nettles and simmer until the nettles are tender. Season, purée and serve with a swirl of yogurt or cream.

Potage Bonne Femme

Purslane is a weed in England but it was a popular vegetable in France, so it's not surprising to find it in some of the famous soups. In most restaurants bonne femme is a rather bland leek and potato soup, but originally it was made with the addition of equal quantities of sorrel and purslane, which gives it a different aspect entirely. If you find purslane, try adding it to a leek and potato soup. Sorrel will give it a slightly acid note.

Vichyssoise

Vichyssoise is a cold version of leek and potato soup, said to have been invented by a French chef working in the Ritz, New York, who remembered his mother's soups. In hot weather Louis Diat and his brother cooled down the soup with milk. Cooked young nettles rather than purslane is suggested for the wild version of Vichyssoise (but if you add sorrel, its acidity will curdle milk). A vivid green soup is the result, suitable for St Patrick's Day in New York.

GREENS

One of the most useful aspects of using weeds is the plentiful supply of edible leaves for green salads and steamed greens, often coming along in spring before garden vegetables are ready to eat. Wild greens, as we have seen, are high in minerals and vitamins. The stronger flavoured ones can be added to yogurt dips. Later in summer when leaves are tougher, most of them can be steamed as a green vegetable.

Weed Salad

Only young and tender leaves are suitable for a salad, so this is mainly a spring recipe. Wash a selection of weeds, enough to fill a salad bowl: chickweed, fat hen, dandelion, mallow, plantain, sow thistle tops, aramanth – anything young and green that you can identify – except nettles, of course. For colour, add nasturtium flowers, calendula marigold petals or daisies. For extra interest, toast sunflower seeds and sultanas in a dry pan; add a little soy sauce, stir until the liquid has disappeared, and allow to cool. Mix the olive oil, soy sauce and lemon juice and shake up, then toss the salad in the dressing. Sprinkle the seeds, sultanas and flower petals just before serving.

The herbalist Gerard tells us that 'raw purslane is much used in salads, with oil, salt and vinegar. It cools the blood and causes appetite.' One popular salad recipe has a lettuce base, with a lemon juice and olive oil dressing; then it's a mix of chopped purslane, marigold petals, borage flowers and chervil.

Green Aramanth and Aramanth

Green aramanth (*Aramanthus viridis*) is a fairly common weed on lighter soils such as in East Anglia, and often appears where the soil is enriched, for example by pig manure, which may be why it is also called pigweed. It is a very good food source for birds, who love the seeds, but we can eat it too.

Aramanth is another edible green, quite mild in flavour and usually found in the warmer months. In Greece it is cooked and dressed with olive oil and lemon juice, and it's a common food in South India. The seeds are small, but they are said to be high in protein, and there are various recipes for making a porridge from them.

In the last few years there has been a revival of interest in aramanth; it's suggested that it might replace kale as a 'trendy vegetable' for chefs. Steam or blanch it, don't cook it for long, and serve it like spinach.

Hedge Bindweed (*Calystegia sepium*)

A member of the convolvulus family, hedge bindweed is a climbing, twisting plant with attractive white or pinkish flowers and heart-shaped leaves. However, although it looks attractive, this is a weed with a smothering and strangling potential that will take over garden beds. Nevertheless, it's another edible plant, rich in starch and sugars. The young leaves can be cooked as a vegetable, while stems and roots should be washed and steamed. As before, if you can't beat it, eat it.

Nasturtium

Nasturtium (*Tropaeolum*) runs as a weed through many gardens, so eating the plants is a form of control. Nasturtium used to be called Indian cress, although it comes from South America.

However, the 'cress' part of the old name is quite accurate, because nasturtium is related to watercress and has the same peppery taste. Use the plant in salads, such as a simple salad of lettuce, fetta cheese and fresh picked nasturtium flowers and leaves. They are just as useful in a fruit salad. You can stuff the flowers with a soft cheese mix.

Nasturtium Seed Capers

Nasturtium seeds are called 'poor man's capers', although true capers are the unopened flower buds of another plant. Pick the seeds when they are still green, and preserve them in a pickle mixture made by boiling up white wine vinegar, salt, an onion, a lemon, a clove of garlic, a few peppercorns and any other spice you like.

They can be used in dips, with soft cheese, in sauces, soups or casseroles – any dish that needs spicing up a little. Some people make capers from nasturtium flower buds. If you're too late to catch the seeds green and they have dried and gone brown, grind them in a pepper grinder as a substitute for pepper.

The benefits of this plant are considerable. In particular it contains a high level of vitamin C.

Watercress

A weed of streams and wet places, watercress (*Nasturtium officinale*) has been an important plant since ancient times. It is now called a 'super food', and is extensively cultivated in many parts of the world because of its valuable vitamins and minerals, particularly vitamin K, which helps the blood to clot and is therefore important for wound healing. It grows well in hydroponic systems, but it can still be found in the wild.

This plant floats because of its hollow stems; it produces little green and white flowers. Watercress was traditionally foraged for in spring when vegetables were scarce, especially by children. Look for it in alkaline water such as a chalk stream.

Health warning: The snag with wild watercress is that it can be contaminated by the liver fluke parasite, which affects sheep and cattle on wet ground, and which can affect humans. The fluke's life cycle includes a stage in a freshwater snail that lurks in watercress beds. Wild watercress should be always washed very thoroughly in clean, running water.

Watercress has a lively, peppery taste, common to cresses, and can be added to soups, salads and dips. Our favourite is watercress sandwiches, made with chopped hard-boiled eggs, wholemeal or rye bread, and plenty of chopped watercress.

Watercress Sandwiches

Hard-boil four free-range eggs; shell and chop

Mix in two tablespoons of plain yogurt and one of mayonnaise

Fold in wholegrain mustard, sea salt and freshly ground black pepper to taste

Add chopped spring onions and the chopped eggs

Arrange the watercress leaves on slices of bread, and cover with the egg mixture.

Common Mallow (*Malva neglecta*)

The leaves and also the seeds of mallow are eaten as a vegetable in many parts of the world, and it's useful as a thickener for soup, because of its mucilage. One plant I observed last year reached a height of over a metre. Pink/mauve five-petalled flowers are followed by pale green seed heads. These are sometimes called 'mallow cheeses' and can be added to savoury dishes, steamed or fried. Once they are brown, they'll be too tough to eat. Mallow can be an ingredient of weed salad or stir-fry greens.

The Book of Job mentions as a hardship that people who were 'driven forth of men' ate weeds including mallow, but it was highly esteemed by the Romans and is still eaten with relish in countries bordering the Mediterranean. Mallow has a long tap root and so is a good source of minerals: calcium, magnesium, potassium, iron and selenium.

Mustard

There are several wild mustards in the cabbage family, some tougher than others. Charlock mustard (*Sinapsis arvensis*) is a common wild vegetable. White mustard (*Sinapsis alba*) produces mustard seeds. The yellow flowers are followed by hairy seed pods, which should be harvested before they burst, just as they are getting ripe. Mustard seeds can be used whole for pickling, or ground and mixed with other foods.

Mustard Sauce

To make mustard sauce, dry roast three tablespoons of seeds first, and pound them in a mortar and pestle. Mix in the following ingredients one at a time:

3 boiled and mashed egg yolks
10 cloves of crushed garlic
1 tablespoon flour
¾ cup wine vinegar
lemon juice
1 teaspoon sea salt

FURTHER RECIPES

Stir Fry Greens

'Costolina', cat's ear or flatweed (*Hypochaeris radicata*) is valued as a vegetable in Sicily. This weed is often called 'false dandelion'; it has similar flowers and wind-borne seeds, but several solid stems rise from the rosette of leaves. True dandelion has a single hollow stem.

The leaves are boiled until tender, then garlic is fried in olive oil for two or three minutes, and the greens are added and stir fried before serving. This treatment works for many wild greens.

Steamed Nettles with Poached Eggs

In a cold spring, steamed nettles with poached eggs was a favourite with us, although the nettles must be young: once the plant flowers, the leaves are too gritty to eat. The grit on mature leaves is an irritant.

Take gloves, scissors or secateurs and a basket to a patch of young nettles. Handle them with care, as the sting is quite painful. (If you are stung, rub the affected skin with a dock or a plaintain

Steamed nettles.

leaf for quick relief.) Cut the tips from the plants. Rinse them carefully in cold water, then steam for a few minutes, chop with butter, arrange on a plate, and top with free-range poached eggs.

Ground Elder Frittata

Since this is a nuisance weed, eating it is a very good idea. Although it may not completely eradicate the plant, regular use should control it from spreading. The leaves have a slight spicy flavour that is not intrusive.

A bunch of young, fresh ground elder shoots, finely chopped
6 free-range eggs
Butter
Salt and pepper
Garlic if you like
Chopped onion and a little chopped bacon (optional)

Beat the eggs and add a little milk. Sauté the onion and bacon in a little butter. Add the beaten egg and seasoning, mix well. Add the chopped ground elder leaves, and pour the mixture into a greased flan tin. Bake until set.

This recipe works just as well with a range of green leafy weeds when they are young.

DRINKS

Elderberry Cordial

Elderberry bushes lined the lanes where we lived, and every September our aunt took us to pick elderberries, to make her famous cordial. She called elder by its old name: the 'bourtree bush'. In the country it had a rather sinister reputation, as the leaves can be poisonous to livestock. Nobody took firewood from an elder tree, either because it was bewitched, or more probably because the wood contains cyanide. The berries are safe, but are always cooked before adding to recipes.

Ground elder frittata: revenge on a troublesome weed.

It was a rich harvest – no wonder elderberries were once grown commercially before imported fruit made its way into England. The purple berries glisten in the sun, with no thorns to protect them. Elderberries can also be made into a deep red wine, but our family stuck to the cordial, relying on it to see them through the winter. We drank it diluted with hot water, as a comforting bed-time drink.

To make the cordial, pull the berries from the stalks with a fork and put them in a saucepan with just enough water to cover them. Simmer for twenty minutes, cool and then strain, pushing the juice through muslin. Measure the juice, and for every half-litre of juice add 400g sugar, and honey to taste. My aunt always added cloves at this stage. Boil for ten minutes, then pour into hot sterilized bottles.

On winter evenings anyone who came in cold from the farm was given elder syrup, diluted with boiling water.

Weed Smoothie

This is a wild version of the blended raw vegetable juice that is a favourite with athletes and a pick-me-up for jaded office workers. It is also recommended for persuading children who hate greens to take in some of their benefits.

To make the smoothie, first chop up a banana and an orange, minus the peel and pips. Then chop a cup of mixed weeds: mine is made with mallow, plantain, fat hen and a little dandelion (purslane would be too strong a flavour). Chop them finely and take out the stems. Blend with the orange and banana until the mixture is smooth.

Nettle Beer

Gather a bucketful of nettle tops, and add three or four handfuls of dandelion leaves and the same of cleavers. Wash them thoroughly, and remove any insects and dead leaves. Then proceed as follows:

Add enough water to cover the nettles. Boil gently for about forty minutes with 60g of

Weed smoothie.

bruised whole ginger, then strain, and stir in a cupful of brown sugar. Let this cool to lukewarm, then spread 30g of yeast mixed up with a spoonful of sugar on a slice of toast. Float the toast on top of the liquid, keep it warm overnight, then remove the scum and stir in a tablespoon of cream of tartar. Bottle and cork.

Other wild herbs used in this beer included burdock, though we never tried it. Another herb beer was made with horehound (*Marrubium vulgare*), a bitter herb used as a tonic and a cough cure.

Borage Lemonade

There are many borage recipes; this plant has a cucumber-like scent and taste, and is often used in cool drinks. When very young the leaves are good in salads, but mature leaves are too rough.

Borage flowers.

To make borage lemonade you will need the following ingredients:

¼ cup lemon juice
2 tablespoons sugar
4 borage leaves
2 cups water

Blend all the ingredients for about half a minute, strain and refrigerate; decorate with borage flowers before serving.

Dandelion Flower Wine

Dandelion flower wine has a pleasant, slightly bitter taste. Place 2 litres of dandelion flower petals into a container, cover with boiling water, and steep for three days. Strain off the liquid, squeezing the flowers and add the zest and juice of four lemons, 680g sugar and 340g chopped raisins. Boil for 20 minutes, cool and then add 15g white wine yeast. Keep in a warm place and in about three days, when bubbling begins, strain and pour into demijohns with a bubble trap. After a couple of months, fermentation ceases and the wine can be put into sterile bottles. Keep a few months before drinking.

Rose-Hip Syrup

Rose hips are another neglected food resource, slowly coming to notice again. The scarlet berries are extremely high in vitamin C, and can be used to make wines, sauces and jellies. Rose-hip syrup was a standard vitamin drink for children in Britain during World War II when fresh fruit was not always available. It's thick and sweet and can be diluted to make a pleasant drink, or used as a topping on ice cream or pancakes. (*See also* rose-hip and crab-apple jelly below.)

To make rose-hip syrup proceed as follows:

Chop 1kg rose hips, add 2 litres water, bring to the boil and simmer for 15 minutes, then leave to cool.
Strain through a cotton cloth in a sieve, and set the juice aside.
Put the rose hips back in the pan with a litre of water, boil as before, and leave to infuse.
Throw away the pulp and combine the two lots of juice, then boil until the liquid is reduced by half.
Stir in 1kg sugar, and boil for five minutes.
Pour into sterilized jars or bottles, and seal.

(Remember to warm the jars or they might crack.)

JAMS AND JELLIES

Blackberries

For generations country women have made blackberry jelly, blackberry and apple jam and blackberry wine, using various popular recipes. We also use blackberries in pies and crumbles, usually with apples because they go so well with them, and the apples dilute the seediness a little. The best quality berries should be used raw, in fruit salad. As you would expect, the best berries are picked early in the season. There are many recipes available, well worth trying because of the very high vitamin C and antioxidant content of the fruit. The ripe berries have a lovely fragrance. Blackberries freeze well, so you can freeze them when picked and enjoy them all the year, or you can make jam later. Just pack them gently into a plastic container and freeze.

Blackberry and Apple Jam
1kg ripe blackberries
1.5kg green apples (Bramley Seedlings are best)
1.5kg sugar

Peel, core and cut up the apples, and simmer with a teacupful of water until tender. Add the blackberries and boil for five minutes, then stir in the sugar. Boil well for about twenty-five minutes. Test the jam on a cold plate – it should set in a few minutes.

Crab-apple Jelly

Crab apples are very acidic in spite of their red cheeks, but with sugar added they make a lovely, clear, rose-pink jelly.

2kg crab apples
500g sugar
Juice of half a lemon

Wash the crab apples and take out any with bruising. Put them whole into a pan and cover with water, then bring to the boil and simmer until they are soft. Pour the pulp into a jelly bag and let it drip through overnight. Avoid pushing the pulp through the bag: when making any fruit jelly, if you do this, the jelly will be cloudy. The next day, measure the juice and add sugar at the rate of ten parts juice to seven parts sugar. Add a little lemon juice and bring to the boil, stirring until the sugar is dissolved. Boil for forty minutes, skimming off the froth.

Put a spoonful in the fridge to test whether it will set. Pour into warm sterile jars and seal while warm.

Crab apples on the tree.

Rose-Hip and Crab-Apple Jelly

This jelly is an even wilder variation. Only wild rose hips are available as a rule, because people rigorously dead-head their tame roses to encourage more flowering.

Wash the rose hips, and again, boil them whole; they take longer than the crab apples to cook, so boil them for thirty minutes before adding the apples, then proceed as before.

Elderberry Ketchup

In some seasons there are more elderberries than enough, and this is the time to make ketchup, using fully ripe elderberries. This was once a popular commercial sauce, known as Pontac's or Pontack sauce. One version is made with claret. A Monsieur Pontac who ran a famous restau-

rant in seventeenth-century London is credited with its invention. The sauce keeps very well – in fact, some say that you should keep it for seven years before using it! This is an excellent sauce to accompany wild game such as venison, and it is also suggested for fish.

2 pints (1.14 litres) ripe elderberries, prepared by stripping them from the stalks and removing the rotten fruit
300ml white wine vinegar or cider vinegar
4 shallots, finely minced
1 teaspoon sea salt
2 teaspoons black peppercorns
2 slices fresh root ginger

Cook the berries in a ceramic dish with the vinegar at about 150°C for half an hour. Leave to soak overnight. Next day strain the juice into a pan, and add the rest of the ingredients. Boil for ten minutes, then sieve. Put into sterile bottles, seal, and store in a cool dark place.

DESSERTS

Puddings from the wild – what a contradiction in terms that seems! But wild nuts and berries can contribute to sweet courses, and are always better when sweetened with honey. Below are a few that we've made over the years, but there are many more for you to invent.

Hazelnut Coffee Cake

Shell the nuts and roast them for about five minutes, then blend until you have hazelnut meal.

(You can buy hazelnut meal if the squirrels have beaten you to the hedgerow.) I learned about making cakes like this from Ruth, a German lady who made a delicious chocolate torte with hazelnut meal. My version is a coffee cake, rather less rich.

115g butter
115g caster sugar
2 eggs
115g self-raising flour
1 dessertspoon instant coffee
50g hazelnut meal

Beat the butter and sugar until creamy. Add the eggs one at a time, beating in with a little of the flour. Fold in the rest of the flour, the coffee and the hazelnut meal. Bake until firm on

Hazelnut cake.

top and shrinking slightly from the edges of the tin. Top with coffee icing.

Serve with whipped cream as a pudding, or with coffee.

Blackberry Fool

2 cups blackberries
½ cup caster sugar
2 cups double cream
½ teaspoon vanilla essence
2 teaspoons lemon juice

Blackberry.

Combine the berries, sugar and lemon juice in a blender. Sieve the purée through a fine mesh, pushing it through to get rid of the seeds. Reserve about ½ cup of purée.

Whip the cream and vanilla until it forms peaks, mix with the berry purée, and refrigerate in serving bowls. To serve, drizzle with the reserved purée and decorate with blackberries.

Wild Summer Pudding

This pudding can be made with any kind of stewed berries, such as blackberries and elderberries combined, or bilberries. In days of yore it was served with custard: now we prefer cream. This pudding was one of my mother's standbys when berries were ripe.

500g berries
85g caster sugar
Slices of white bread
Dusting of cinnamon

Simmer the berries with the sugar in the minimum of water needed to keep them from sticking to the pan. Cut the crusts off the bread, and dust the slices with cinnamon. Line a bowl with clingfilm and then with slices of bread, ensuring the entire surface is covered. Add a third of the cooked berries, then another layer of bread, repeat and finish with a layer of bread. Put a plate on top with a weight on it. Refrigerate overnight and turn upside down to serve.

10 SAFETY

Obviously it is crucial to identify plants correctly. One or two of our common weeds can be dangerous, and a few can be poisonous to us and to farm animals. Goats seem to be particularly vulnerable to poisonous plants, but perhaps this is because they are curious and nibble at plants that other animals wouldn't touch. Of course, we live with poisons in plants and have learned to avoid them. You will know that the leaves of the potato plant are poisonous, as are rhubarb leaves. Even potatoes are bad for you if they turn green in sunlight, which is why we keep them in the dark.

It is unwise to handle plants if they could be contaminated with chemical sprays.

Even if you don't use sprays yourself, spray drift in rural areas can travel on the wind and settle on your land.

Petty spurge (*Euphorbia peplus*) is quite common in gardens. It has lime green leaves, reddish stems and a white corrosive sap in the stem that

Petty spurge.

is used to treat skin cancer spots, but which can blister your skin and is dangerous if it gets into your eyes. This plant is quite similar to **chickweed** (*Stellaria media*), a plant often used in salads, as mentioned. The sap of petty spurge is useful in clearing small skin cancers, but it must be treated with great respect.

Hemlock (*Conium* spp.) is famously poisonous. Socrates was found guilty of corrupting the youth of Athens by asking them philosophical questions, and was given a hemlock drink as a death sentence. The crushed leaves smell foul, but the plant could possibly be confused with **hedge parsley** (*Torilis*), or with **wild carrot** (*Daucus carota*), sometimes called Queen Anne's lace, a plant that lines some of our country roads in summer.

Poisonous plants can pop up where they are least expected. I hadn't seen a thorn apple (*Datura* species) for so many years that it took me a little time to identify it when one turned up in a garden bed. This striking annual plant has large serrated leaves, the trumpet-like flowers and leaves coming straight out of the stem together. All parts of the plant are poisonous, especially the seeds, which are covered in a thorny case. It smells foul, which should deter people and animals from eating it.

The poison in this case is very similar to that of **deadly nightshade** (*Atropa belladonna*), and one of its actions is to dilate the pupils of the eyes. It also causes hallucinations. *Datura stramonium* was used for hundreds of years to relieve asthma, due to its atropine and as a painkiller during sur-

Thorn apple.

Buttercups: pretty but poisonous.

gery, but a fatal dose is quite close to a medicinal dose.

EAT WEEDS WITH CAUTION

Weeds are a source of many types of food. 'Food foraging' is a popular pastime in some of our leafier urban areas, and there are guided walks run by botanists to help you to recognize edible wild plants.

Wild varieties of vegetable are often stronger in flavour than cultivated ones. They often contain more vitamins and minerals, but also more of the potentially toxic constituents. Nitrates and nitrites are present in many plants, and are used as a preservative for meat, because they inhibit the growth of the bacteria that cause botulism.

In general, we are advised that children should not eat excessive amounts – but it seems that the presence of vitamin C in plants will inhibit harmful effects, which explains why we can get away with it.

Oxalic acid levels in wild plants are also often higher than in cultivated ones. The levels are high in many common foods, such as rhubarb, spinach and parsley; in fact most green plants contain some oxalic acid. People with gout are advised to limit their oxalic acid intake. The moreacidic type of wild plant is likely to be high in oxalic acid, weeds such as dock, oxalis and purslane.

Care should be taken to ensure that anything you eat has not been contaminated by bird or animal droppings.

St John's wort.

EXAMPLES OF POISONING BY WEEDS

My own experience of plant poisoning, over many years, is of plants that are not common weeds; however, all these plants are found in gardens.

Buttercups (*Ranunculus acris*) are common in meadows, but the sap can cause blisters. Fortunately the plants are harmless when dried and made into hay.

St John's wort (*Hypericum perforatum*) is a shrub with a yellow flower. It is used by herbalists, but is sometimes responsible for cases of photo-sensitization in cattle – that is, sensitivity to light. This is a common effect of poisonous plants. We had one such case, a black and white Friesian cow that lost all the hair on the white patches of her skin, and the skin itself blistered. She was kept indoors for weeks and treated with gentian violet, a purple dye used to prevent infection.

Also when our family farmed in Wales we had two cows that died in convulsions: this was attributed to foxglove plants, growing in the bottom of the stone walls.

Elderberry bushes (*Sambucus*) provide purple berries that are edible when cooked, and the flowers can be used to make skin preparations. An elderberry cordial rich in vitamin C was an old tradition, to be administered in hot water for colds and flu. However, we found that the rest of the plant is poisonous when one of our goats ate the leaves and died: the leaves contain a glycocide, which gives rise to cyanide in the process of digestion, and cyanide can then build up to toxic levels.

The same cyanide effect can produce poison in the leaves of *Prunus* species.

Wild apple and plum trees are common in some places as weed trees, often where small farms have been amalgamated into larger units of land.

They are a wild resource and we gather the fruit. But if the leaves are wilted, because of damage or frost, their glycocide changes to hydrocyanic acid (prussic acid) and sugar – sweet, but deadly to grazing animals.

(Wild plums and apples can make a valuable contribution to the diet when the fruit is ripe. The malic and tartaric acid in apples aids the digestion and also helps to clean the teeth.)

A FEW OF THE UK'S MOST INVASIVE PLANTS

Giant Hogweed (*Heracleum mantegazzianum*)

This plant was brought into Britain from Southern Russia in the nineteenth century; at about 3 metres high it's an impressive plant. The sap causes blisters and even scars on the skin. This plant is widespread, it spreads by seeds, and you can often see it along riverbanks, where it can choke out native plants and reduce wildlife habitat.

It's illegal to plant giant hogweed, and if you have one on your land you are expected to get rid of it. Digging it out is an option, but cover up first and wear a mask. If possible, it's good to burn poisonous plants. Chemical control by applying glyphosate is the alternative.

Japanese Knotweed (*Fallopia japonica*)

This invader came from East Asia and is hard to eradicate because of its strong, deep roots, by which it spreads. It's an offence against the 1981 Wildlife and Countryside Act to grow it. A biological control method is on trial, using plant-sucking bugs. Let's hope the bugs win!

Himalayan Balsam (*Impatiens glandulifera*)

I've seen this one on shady riverbanks. It spreads by means of many seeds – dig it out before it sets seed if it comes your way, even though the flowers are a pretty pink.

Himalayan balsam.

Common Rhododendron (*Rhododendron ponticum*)

Until fairly recently this shrub was popular in gardens, especially on acid soils. But it makes a habit of escaping, and is now on the black list. It will smother native plants, is toxic to grazing animals and reduces wildlife in its vicinity. It is certainly a menace in native woodland.

END NOTE

There are many more weeds to investigate than the ones in this book. It will be interesting to watch the status of our wild plants in the future: many wild flowers that were once pasture weeds are now cherished in gardens. As we've seen, our weeds can be enjoyed in various ways, and many of them are beautiful.

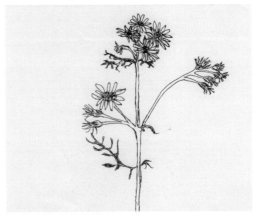

Ragwort.

Wild rose bush in bloom.

Roadside weeds.

FURTHER INFORMATION

BOOKS

Goulson, Dave, *A Sting in the Tale* (Cape, 2013)
A readable account of Professor Goulson's work
with bumblebees and their need for weeds.

Grieve, Mrs M., *A Modern Herbal* (1931,
reprinted many times by many publishers)
This book is probably the most quoted of the
herbals and contains notes from most of the
famous earlier writers.

Griggs, Barbara, *Green Pharmacy; The History
and Evolution of Western Herbal Medicine*
(Healing Arts Press, 1997)
This is a thorough, scholarly and sometimes
horrifying account of herbal medicine through
the ages.

Lewis-Stempel, John, *Meadowland, the private
life of an English field* (Doubleday, 2014)
Carefully observed and beautifully written,
this book gives an insight into the wildlife of a
meadow.

Lewis-Stempel, John, *Foraging, a practical guide
to finding and preparing free wild food* (Constable
and Robinson, 2012)

Phillips, Roger, *Wild Food, A Complete Guide for
Foragers*, revised edn (Pan McMillan, 2014)

Wong, James, *Grow Your Own Drugs* (Collins,
2009)
Recipes for natural remedies.

ORGANIZATIONS

Plantlife
Founded in 1989, this charity speaks up for wild
flowers, plants and fungi.

Plantlife
14 Rollestone Street
Salisbury
Wiltshire
SP1 1DX

Tel: 01722 342730
E-mail: enquiries@plantlife.org.uk
www.plantlife.org.uk

The Bumblebee Conservation Trust (BBCT)
Bumblebee conservation. Numbers have
declined dramatically in the last 80 years but
the insects now have support. This organization
spreads information about bumblebees, their
important role in pollination and what can be
done to help them.

Bumblebee Conservation Trust
Beta Centre
Stirling University Innovation Park
Stirling
FK9 4NF

E-mail: enquiries@bumblebeeconservation.org
www.bumblebeeconservation.org

DEFRA (Department for Environment, Food and Rural Affairs)
Many aspects of rural life including invasive weeds and countryside access.

DEFRA
Nobel House
17 Smith Square
London
SW1P 3JR

Tel: 03459 33 55 77
E-mail: defra.helpline@defra.gsi.gov.uk
www.gov.uk

WEBSITES

www.eatthatweed.com
The Weed Forager's site.

www.goodbugs.org.au
Beneficial insects.

www.earnshawsherbaldispensary.co.uk
Information on natural medicines – including some weeds.

www.rbst.co.uk
Rare Breeds Survival Trust; information about traditional British breeds of livestock.

INDEX

31901063026571